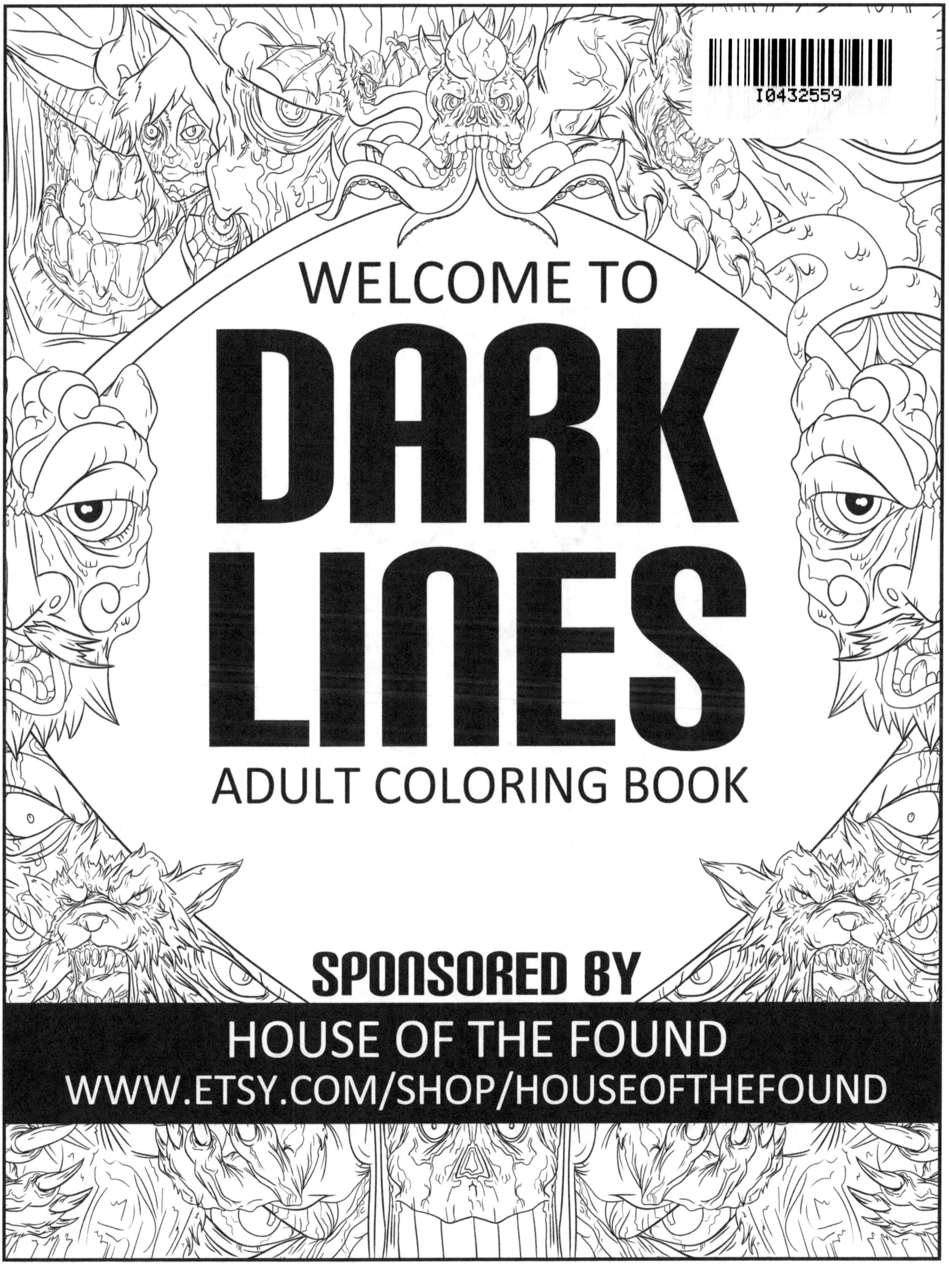

WELCOME TO

DARK LINES

ADULT COLORING BOOK

SPONSORED BY

HOUSE OF THE FOUND

WWW.ETSY.COM/SHOP/HOUSEOFTHEFOUND

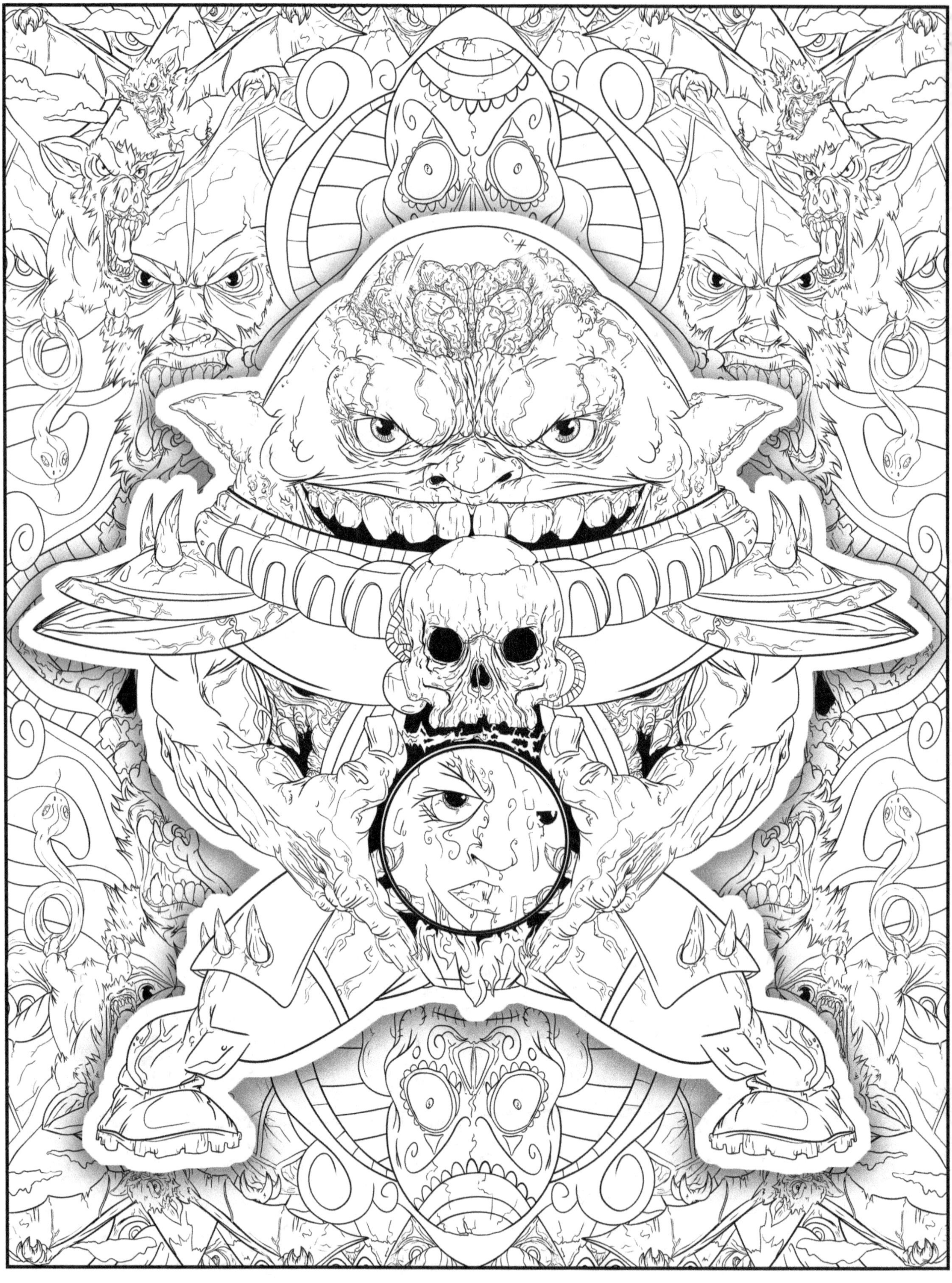

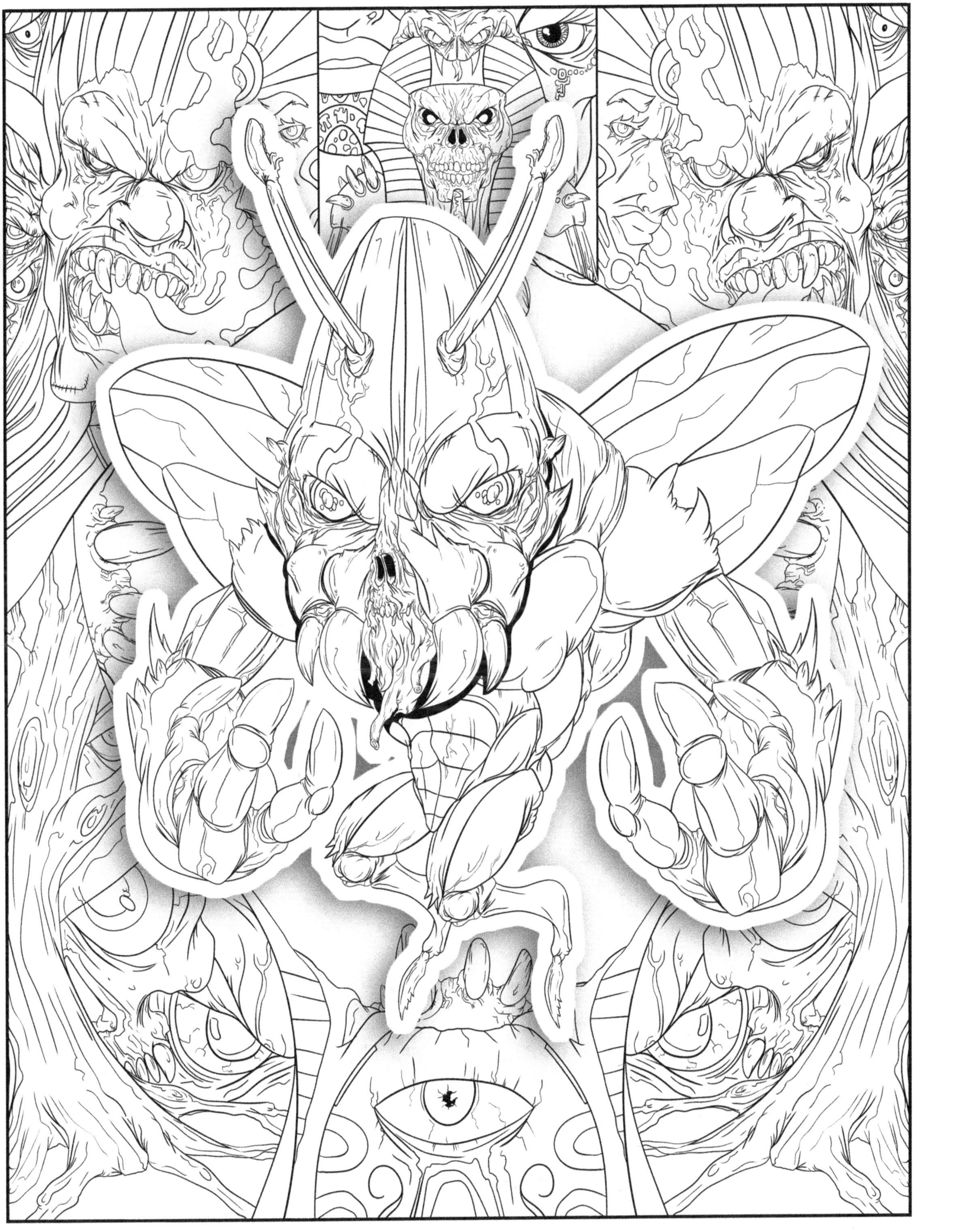

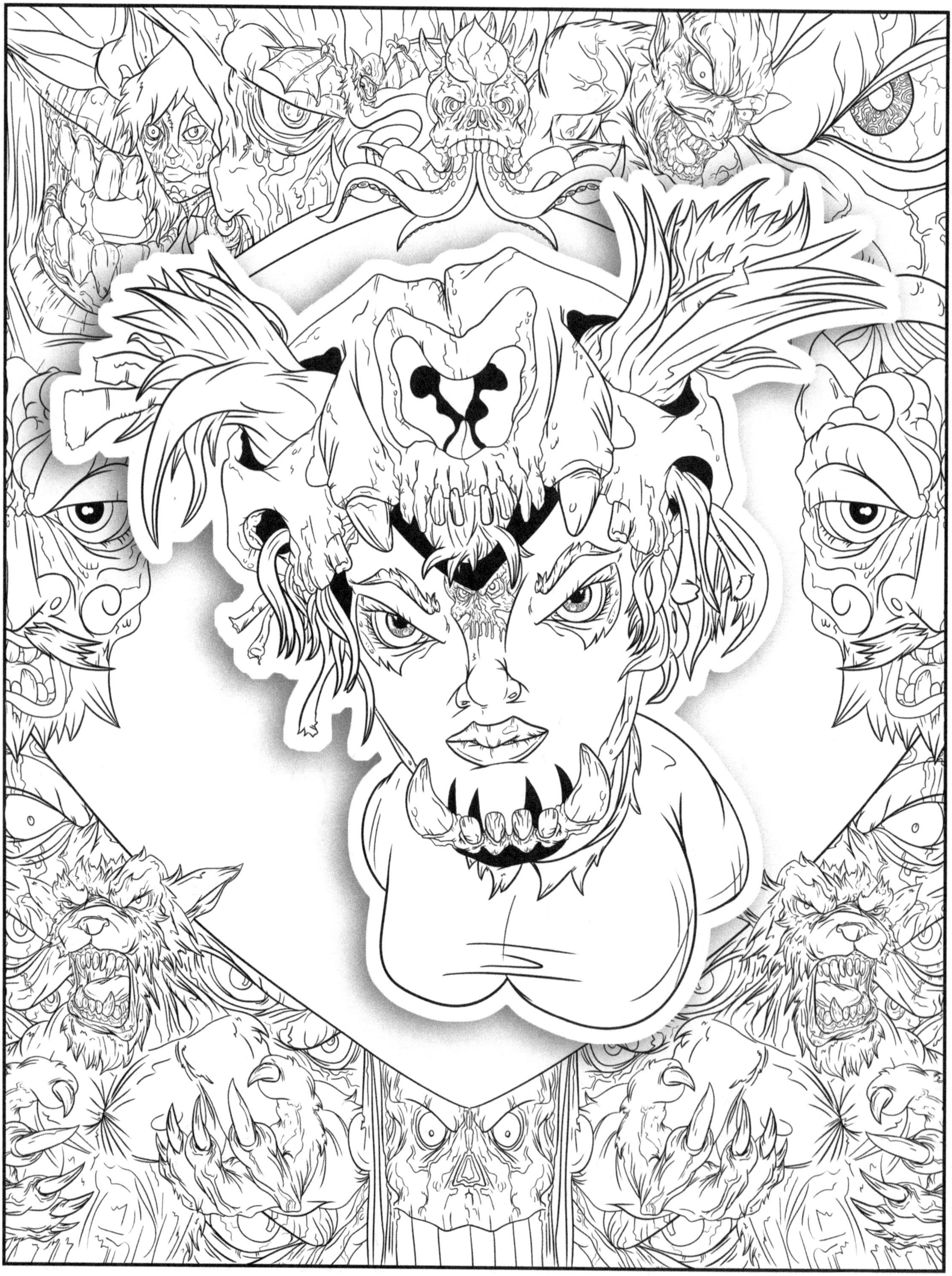

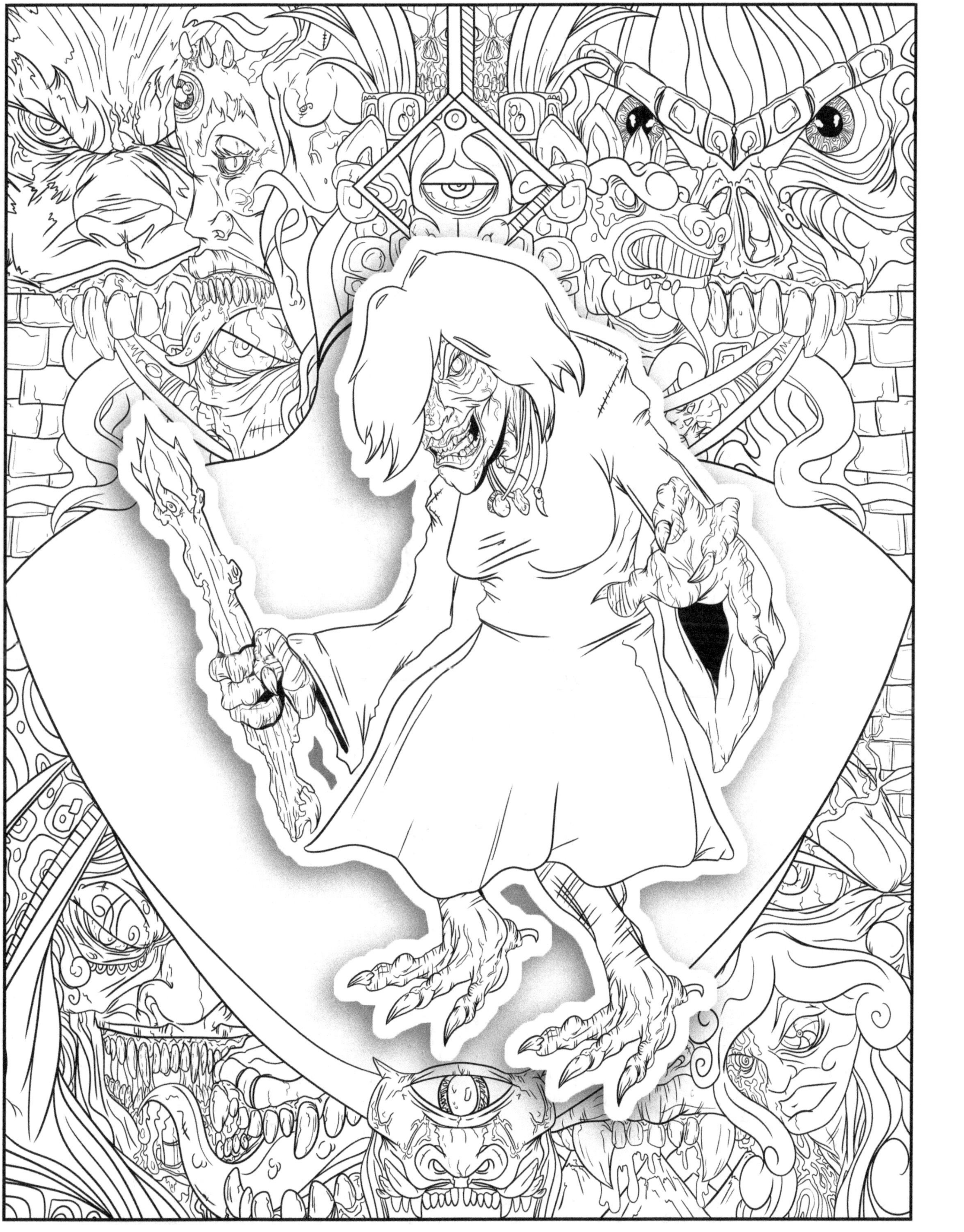

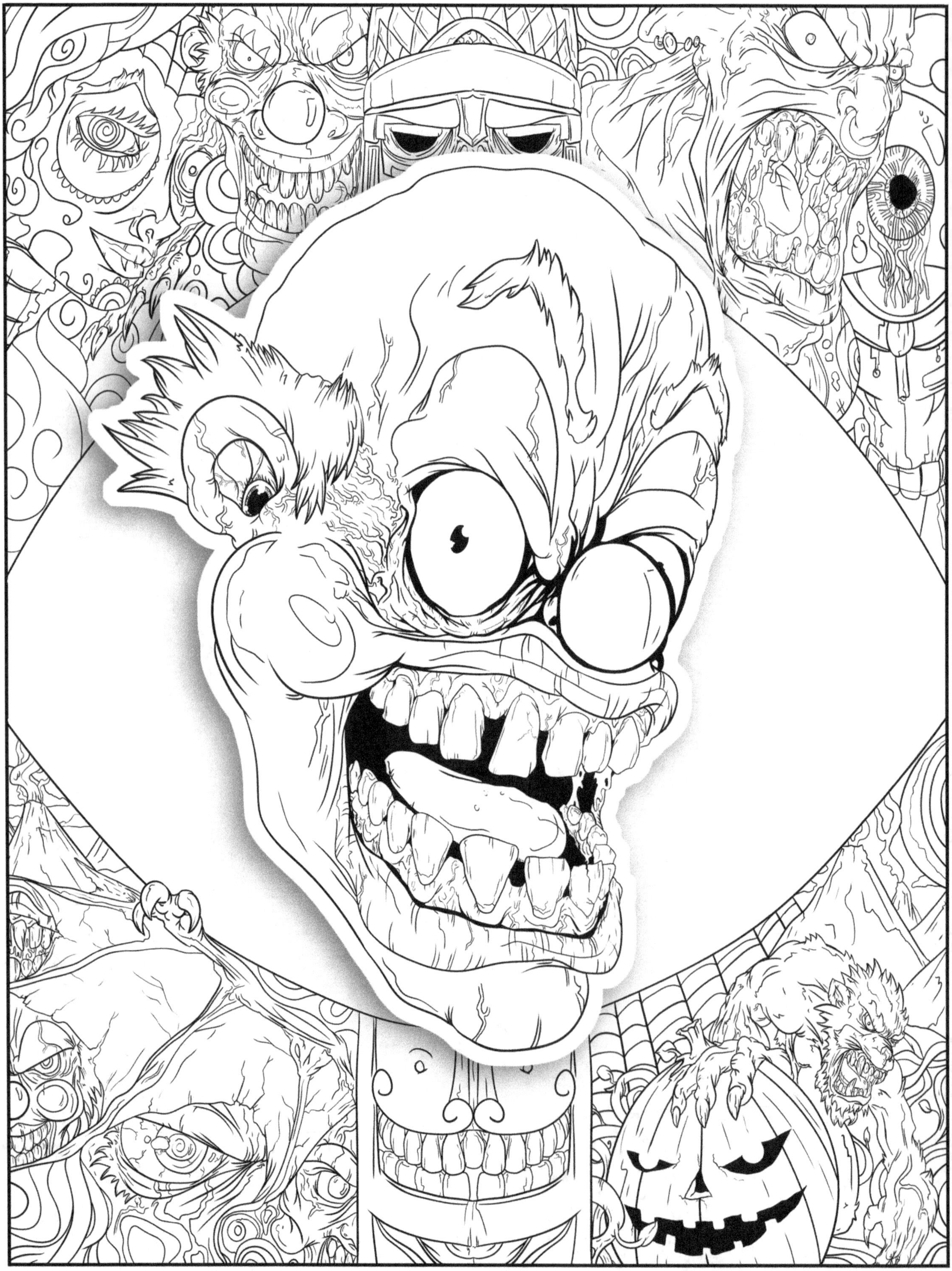

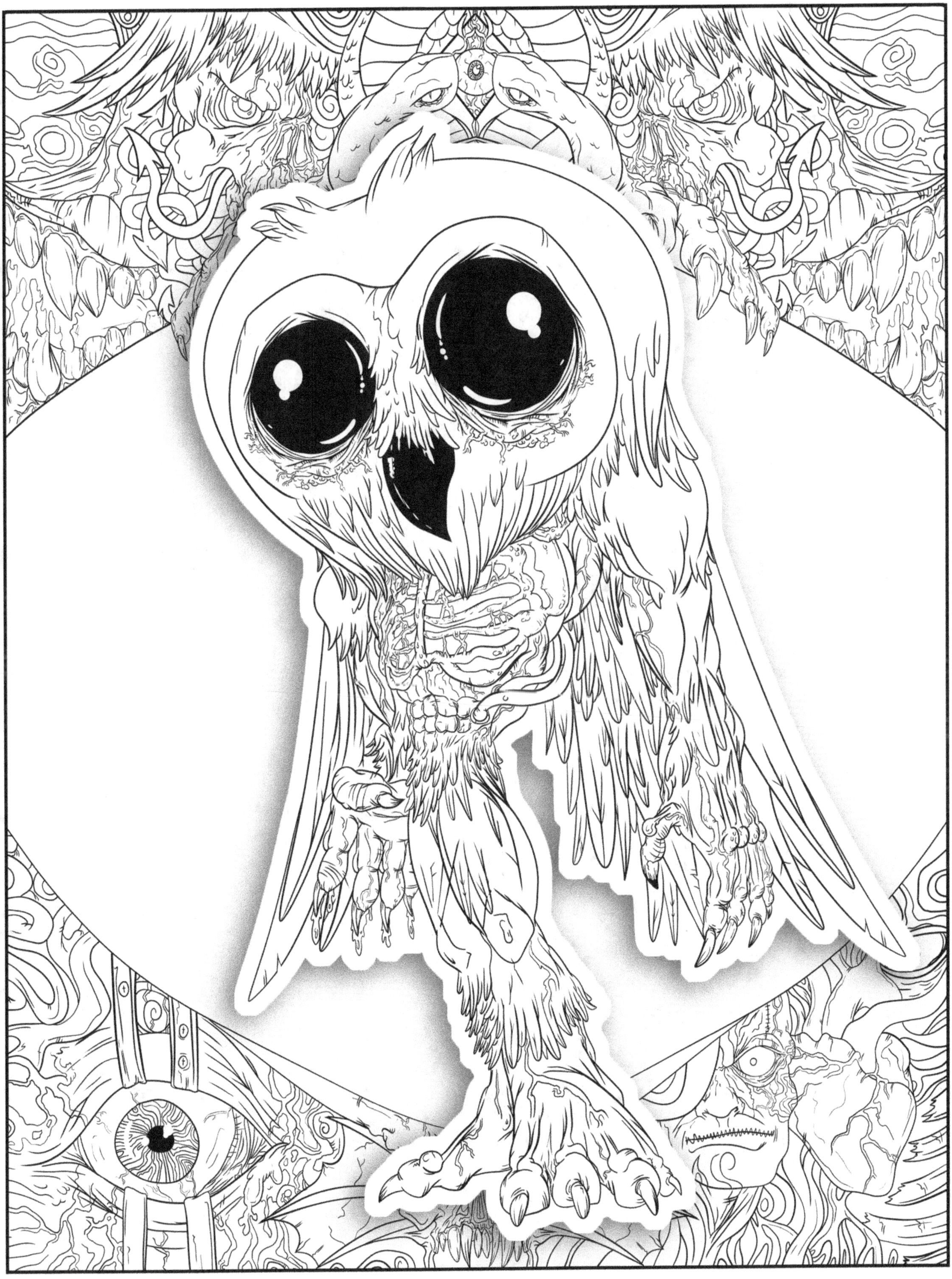

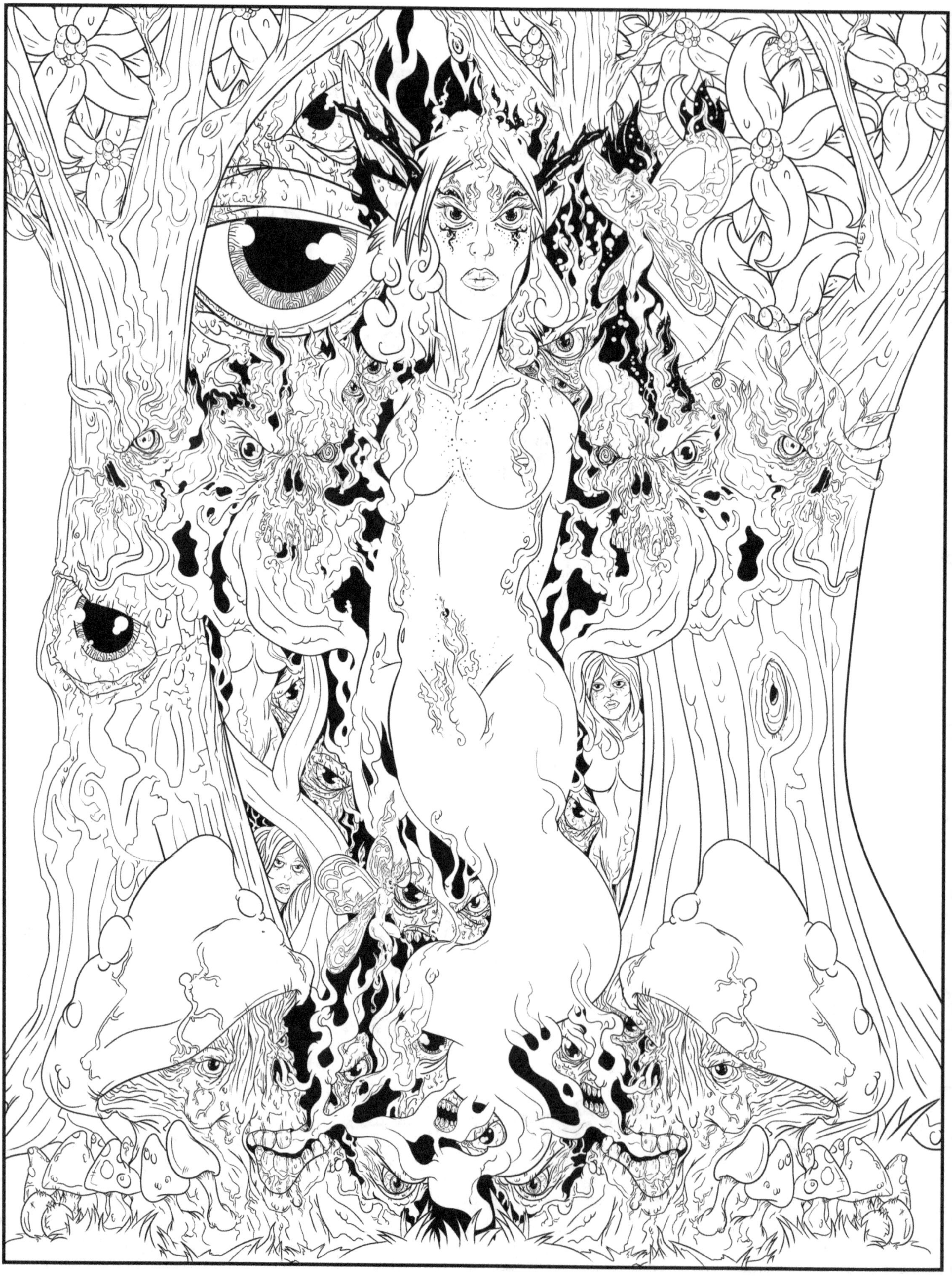

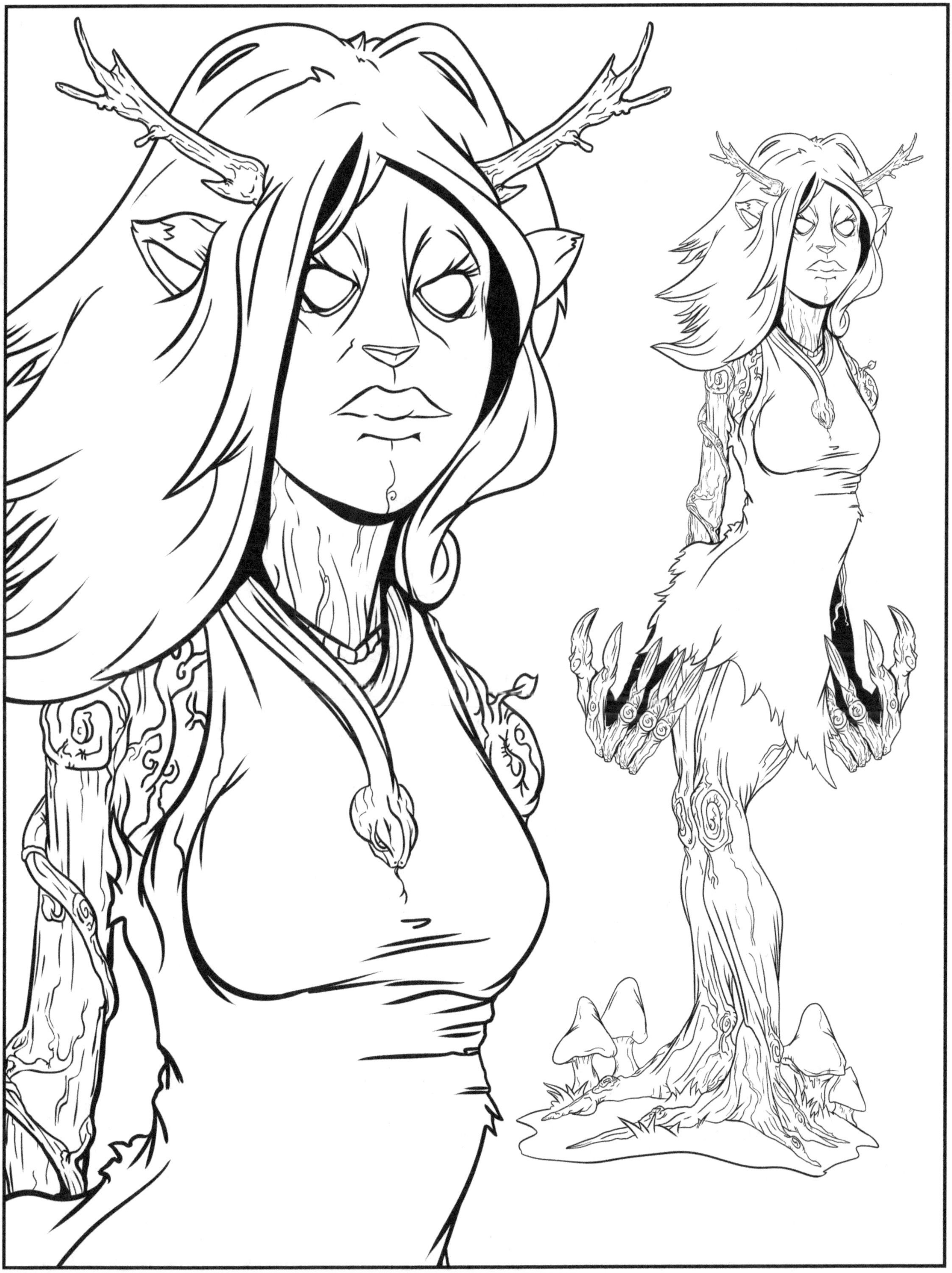

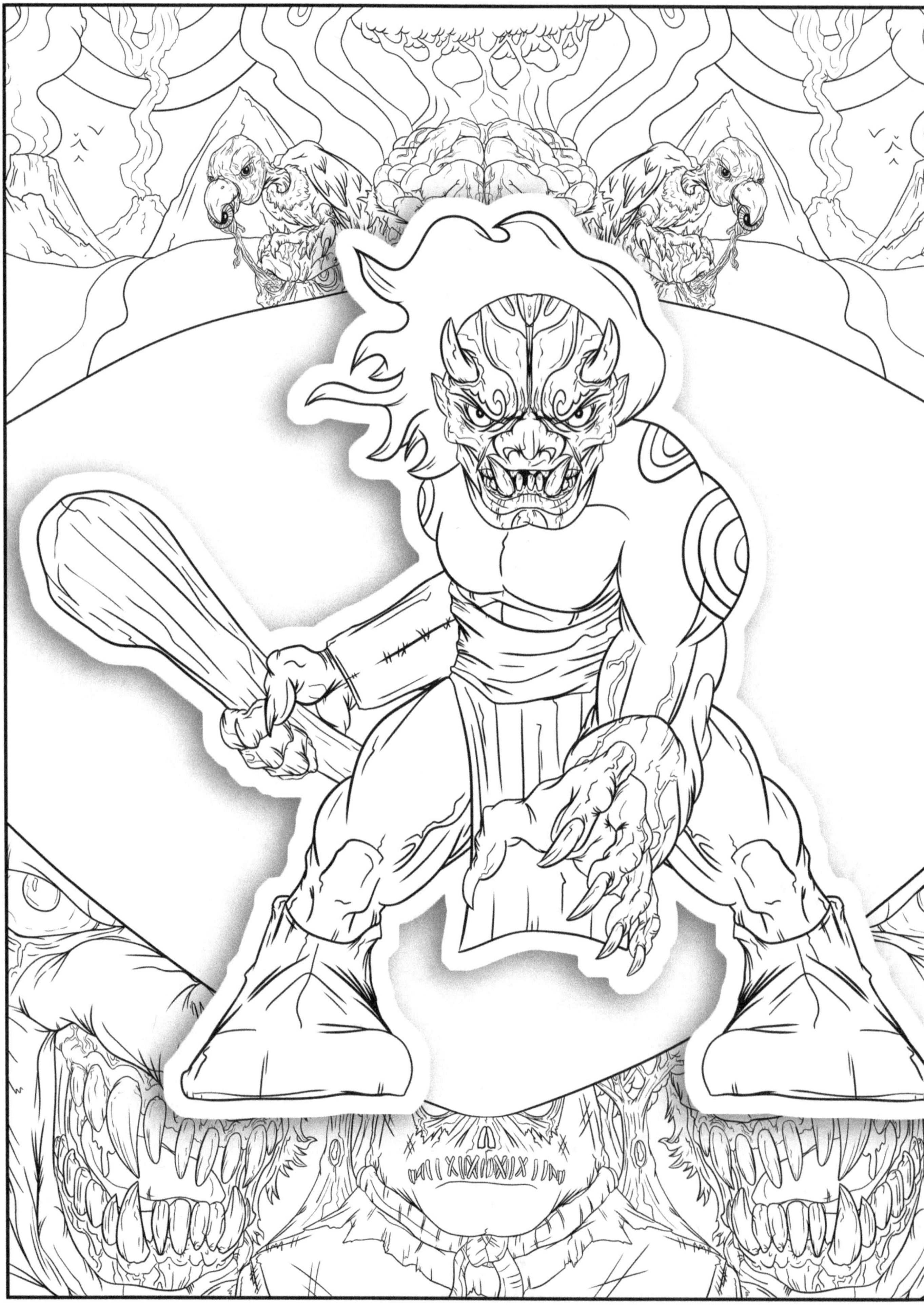

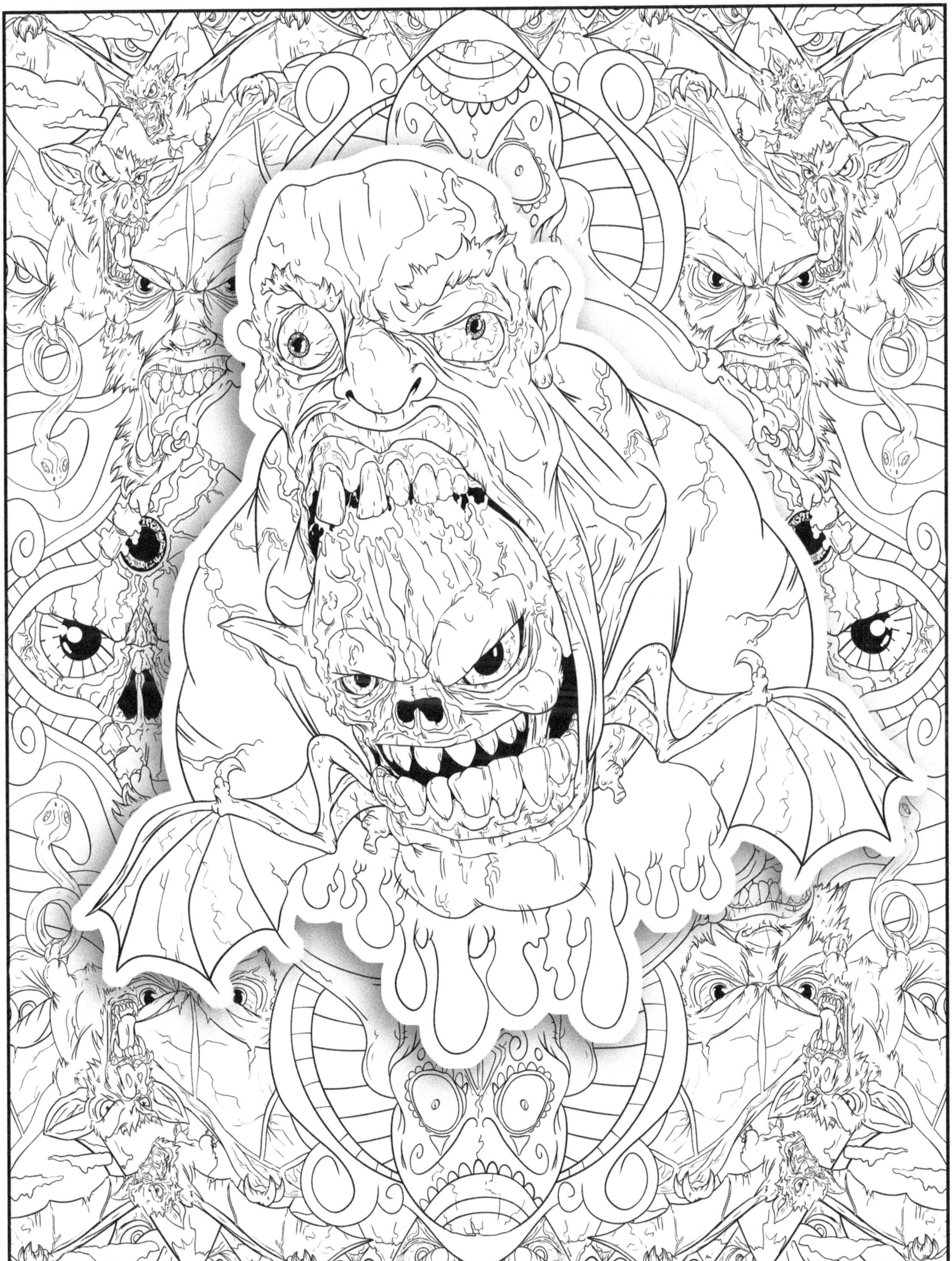

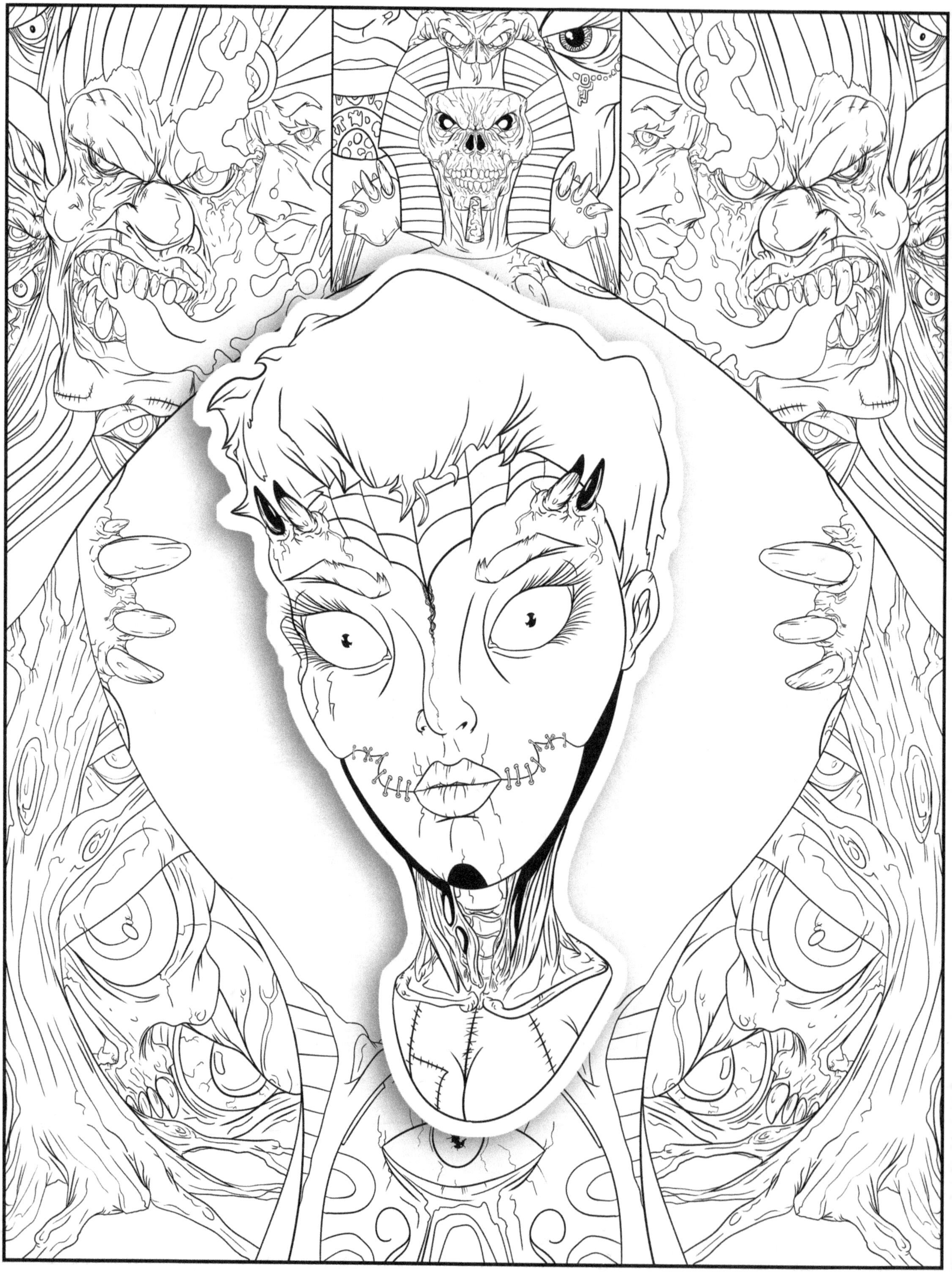

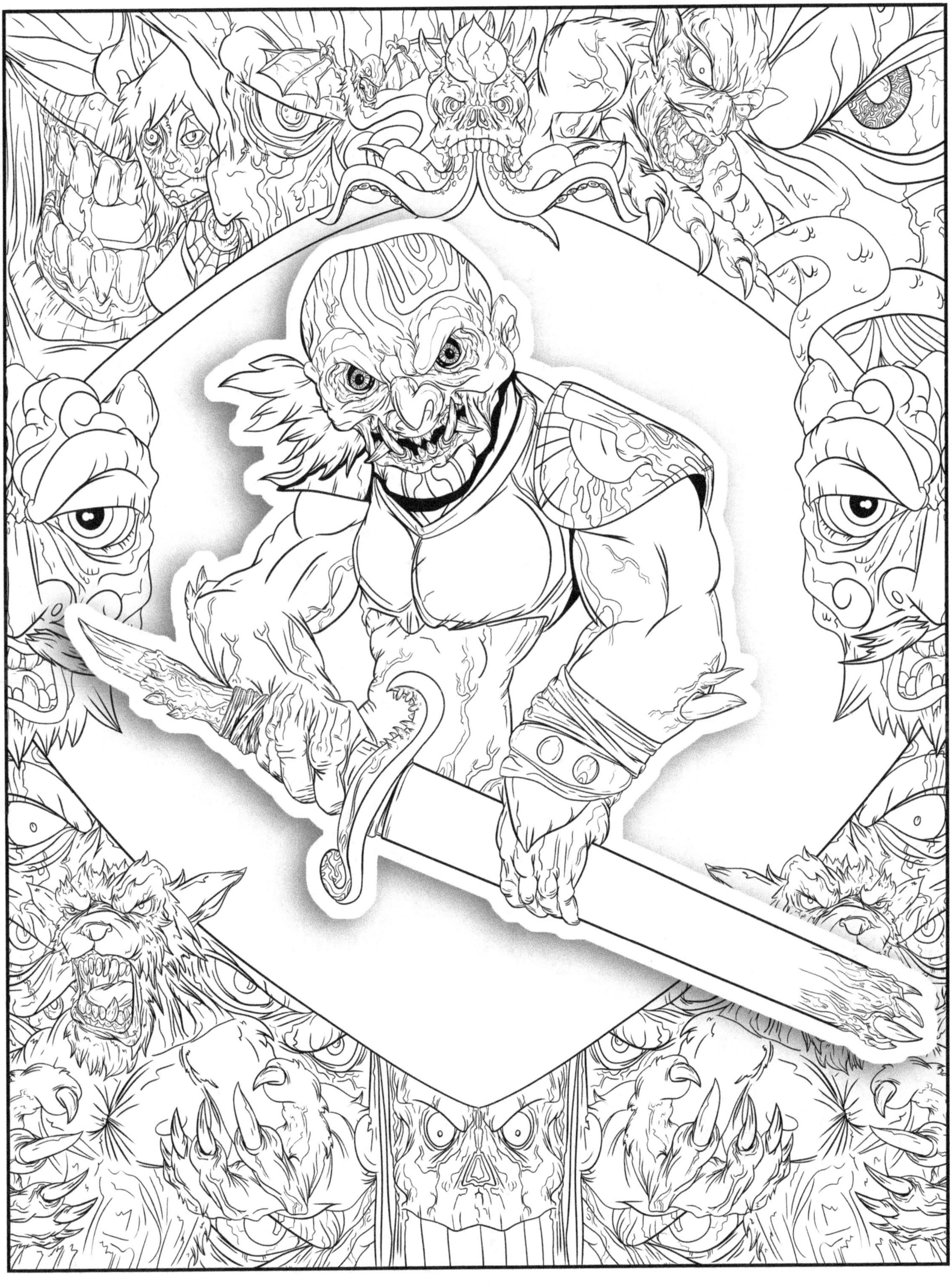

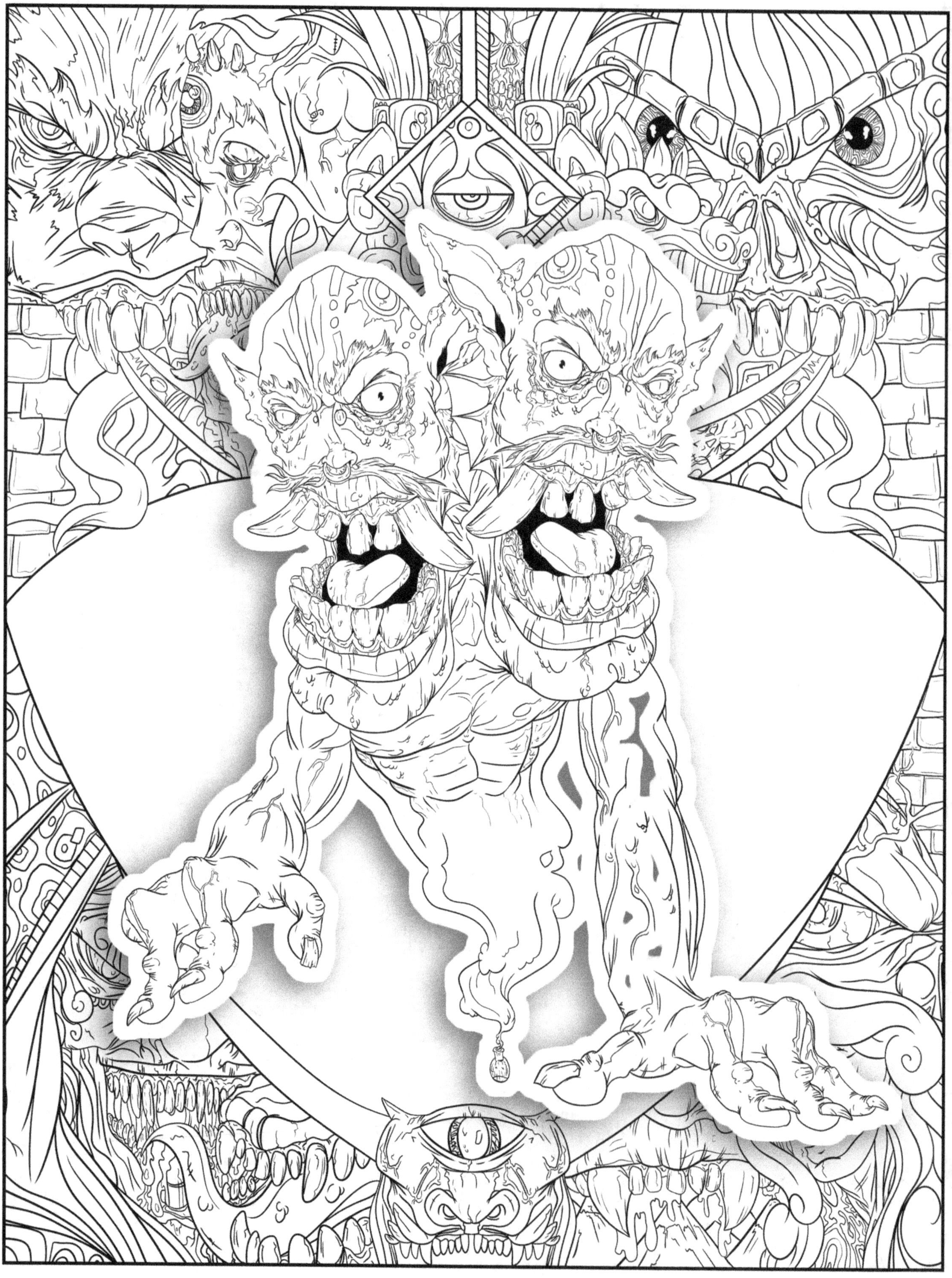

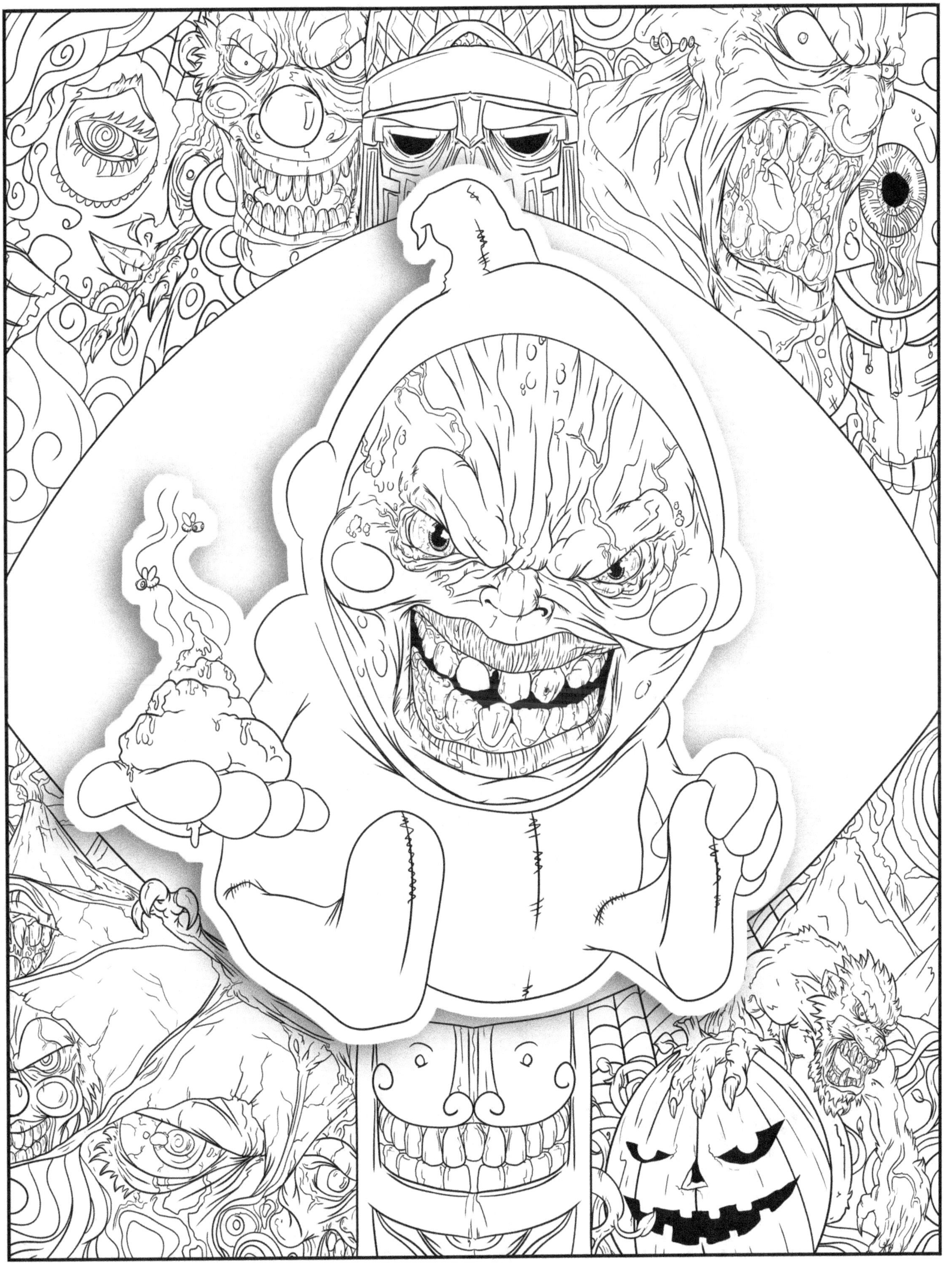

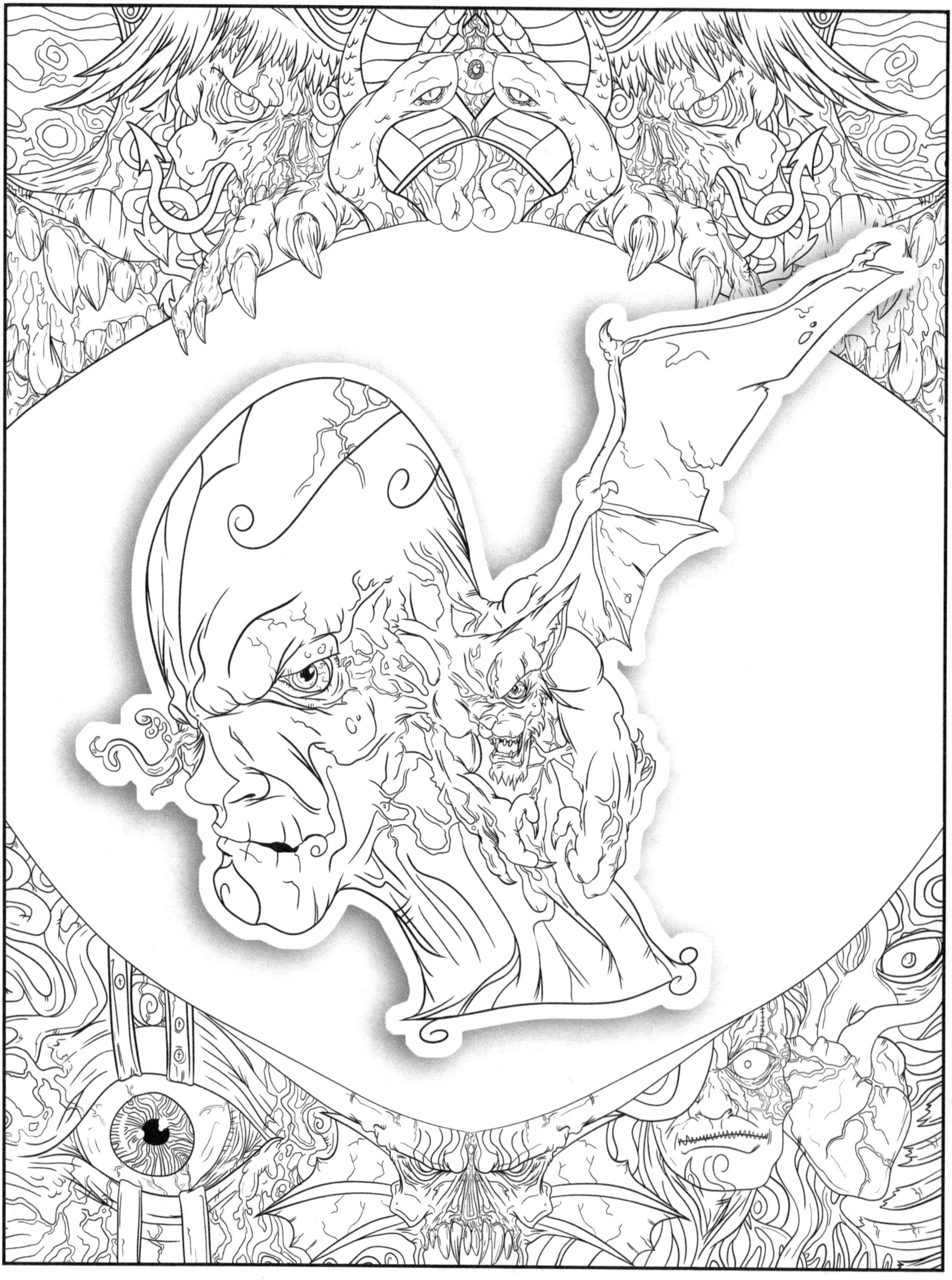

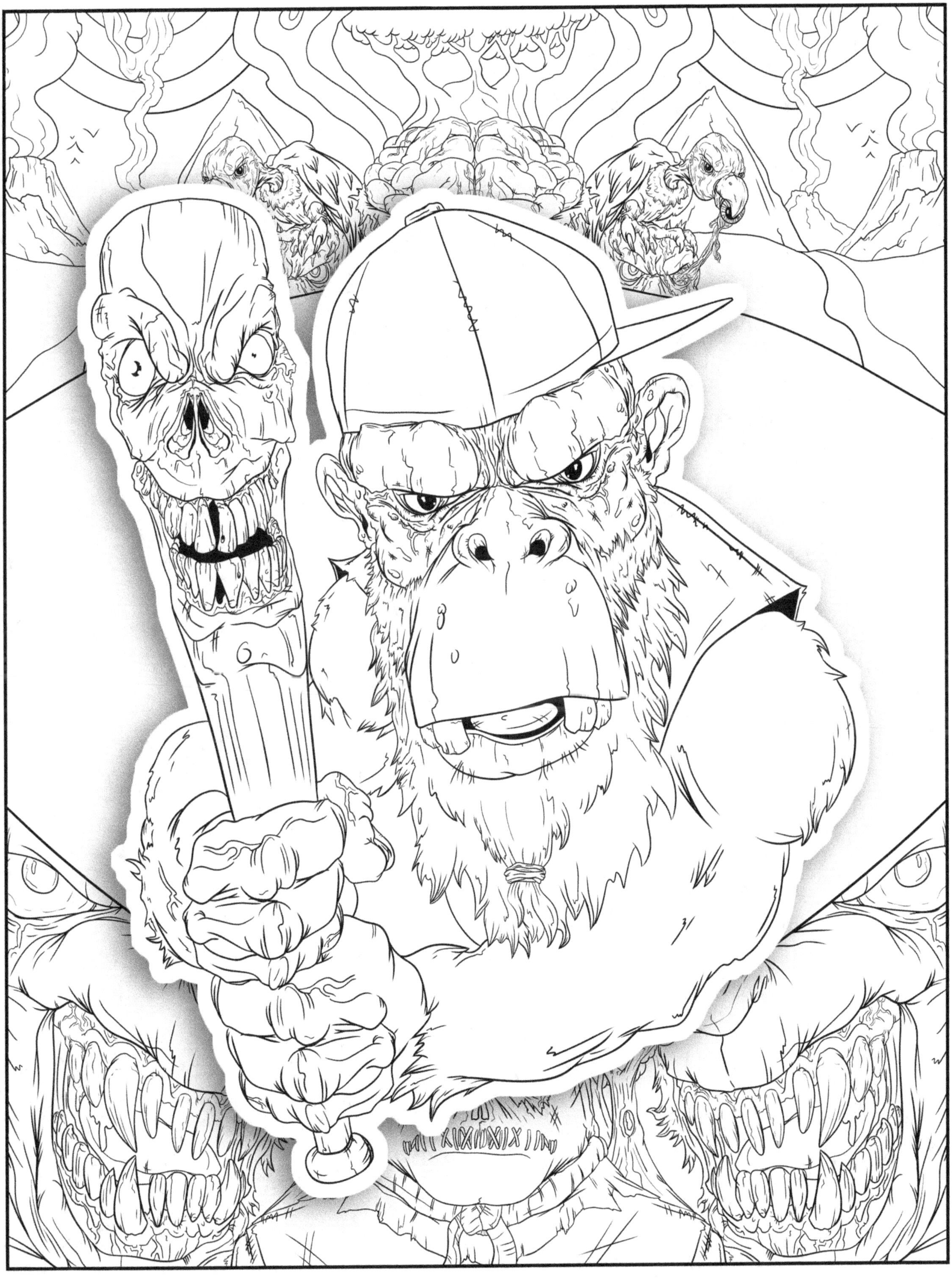

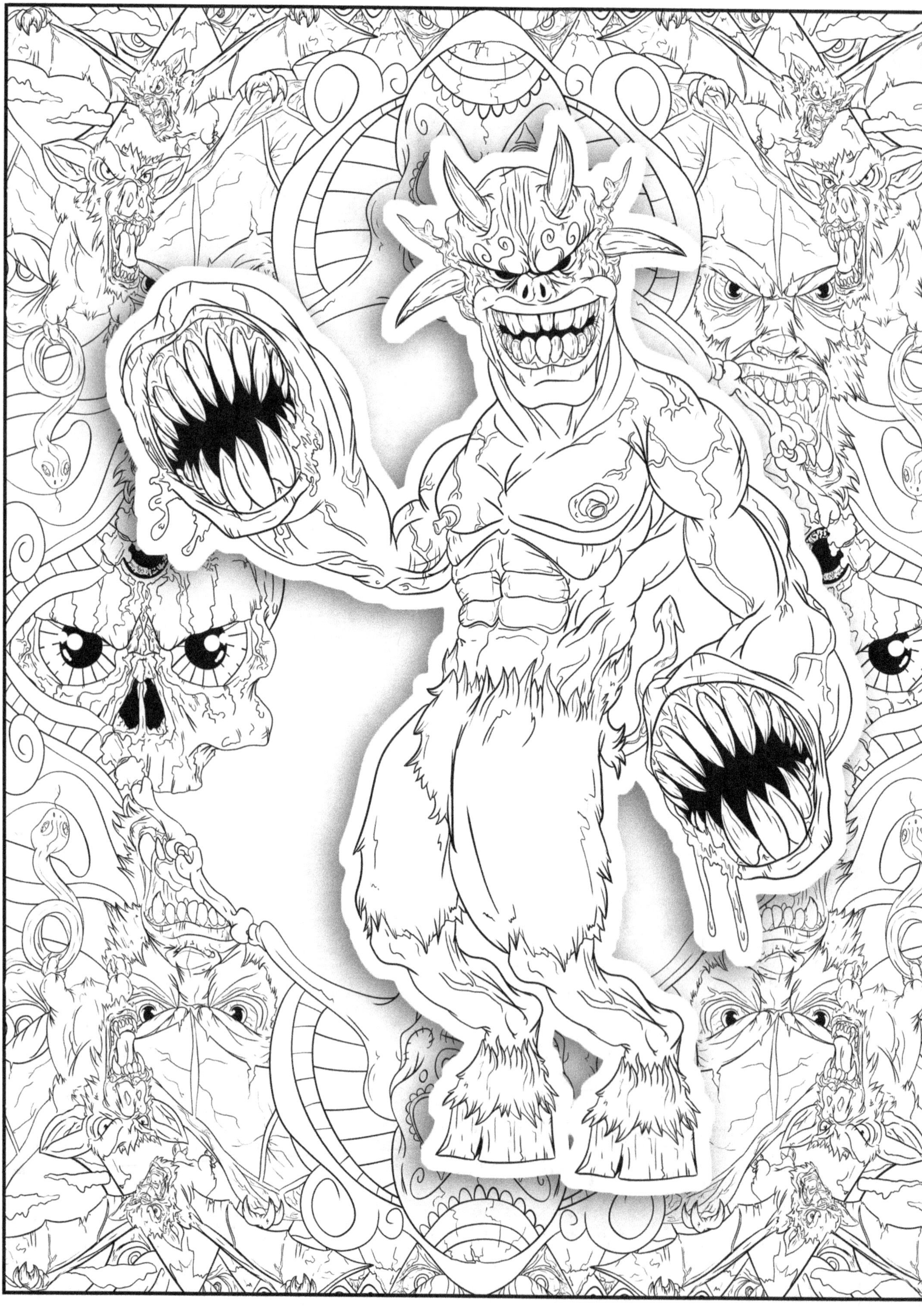

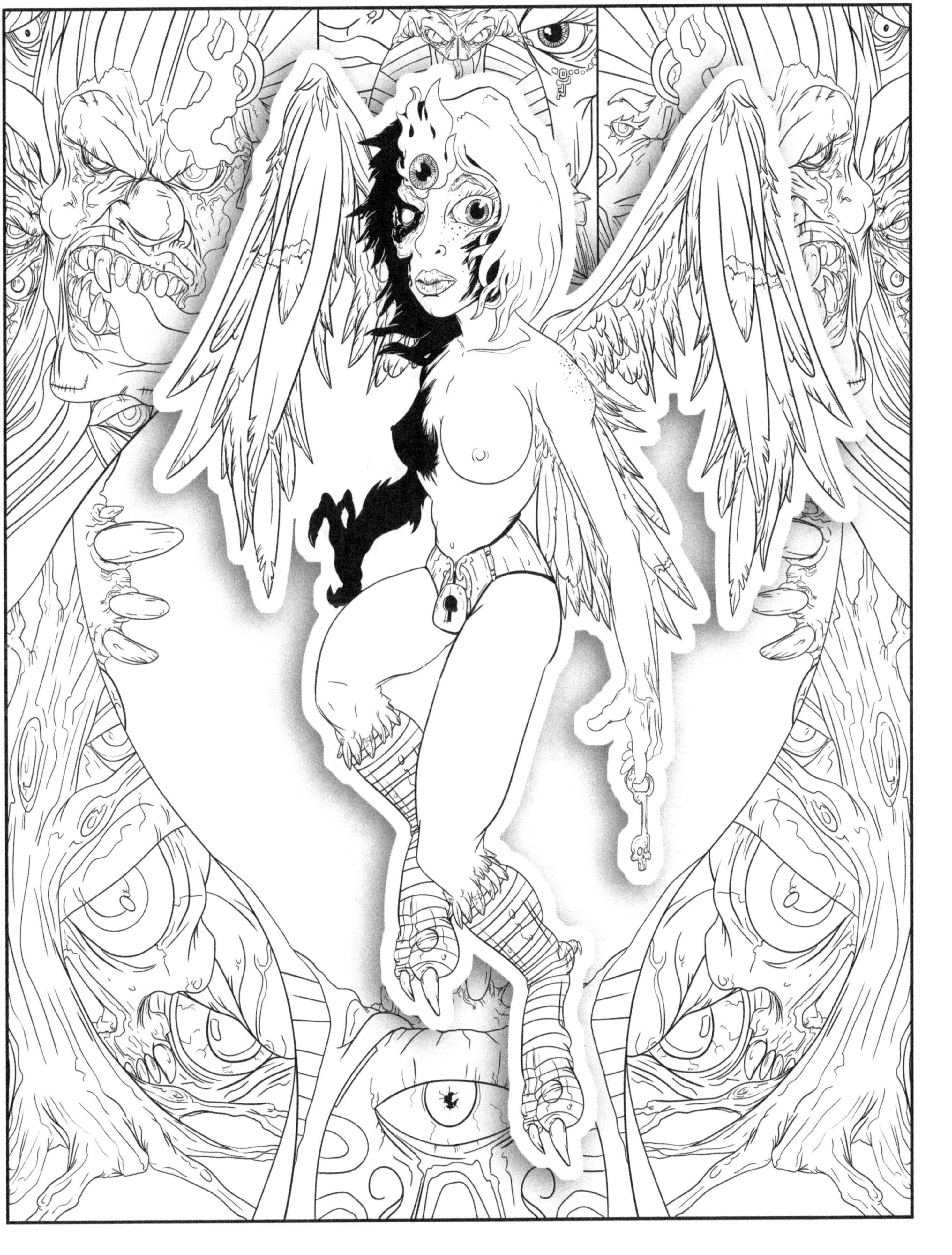

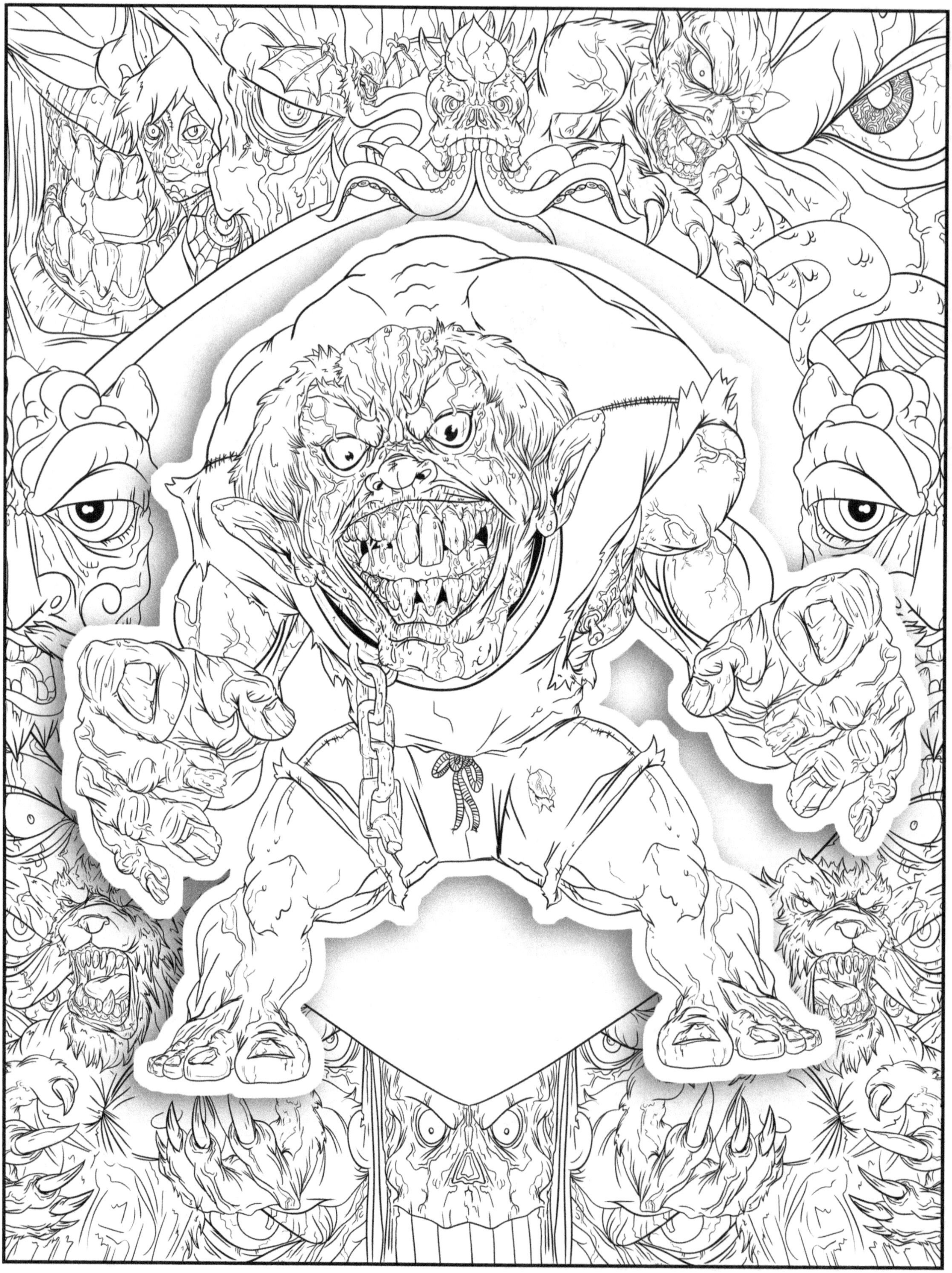

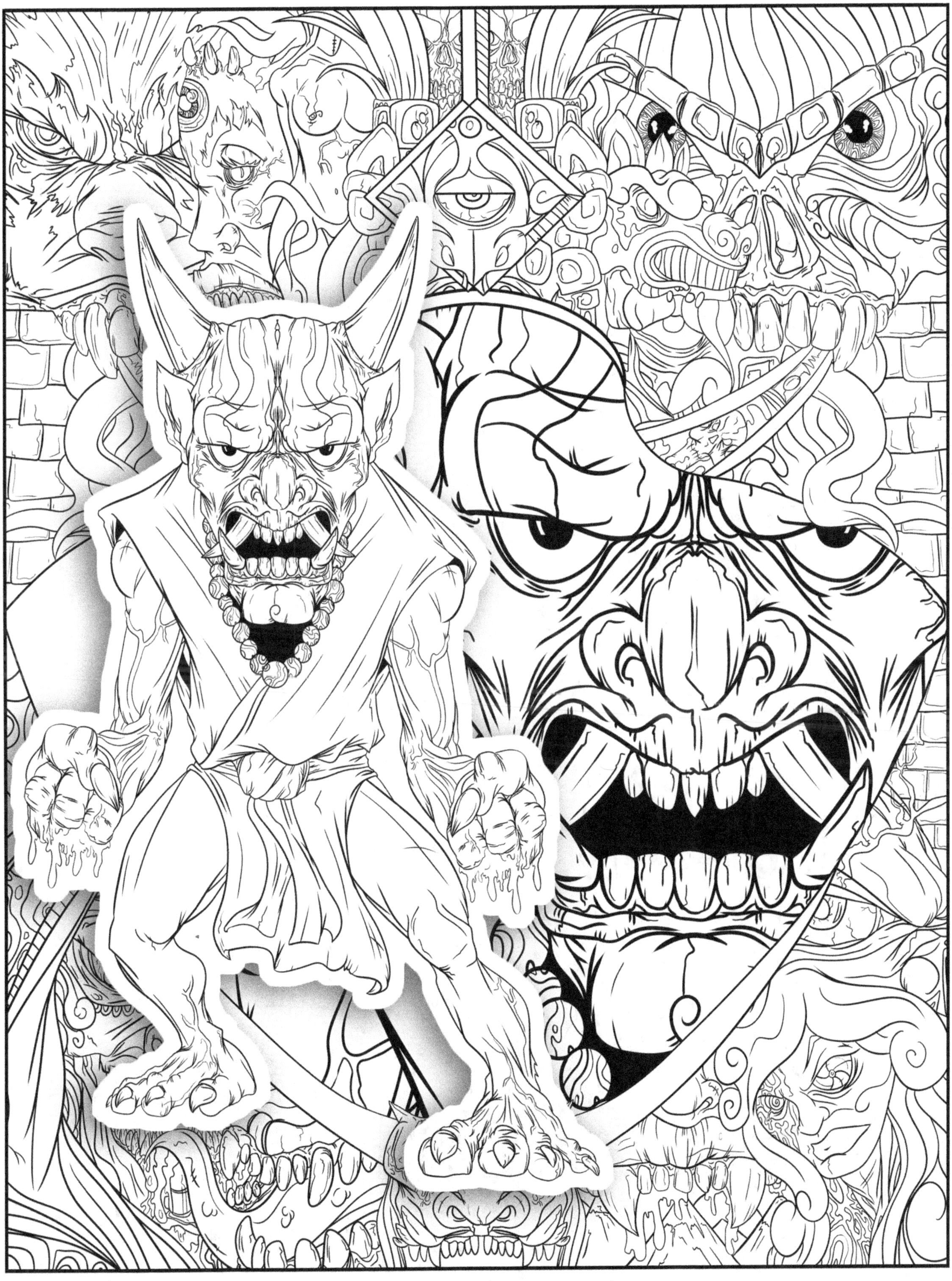

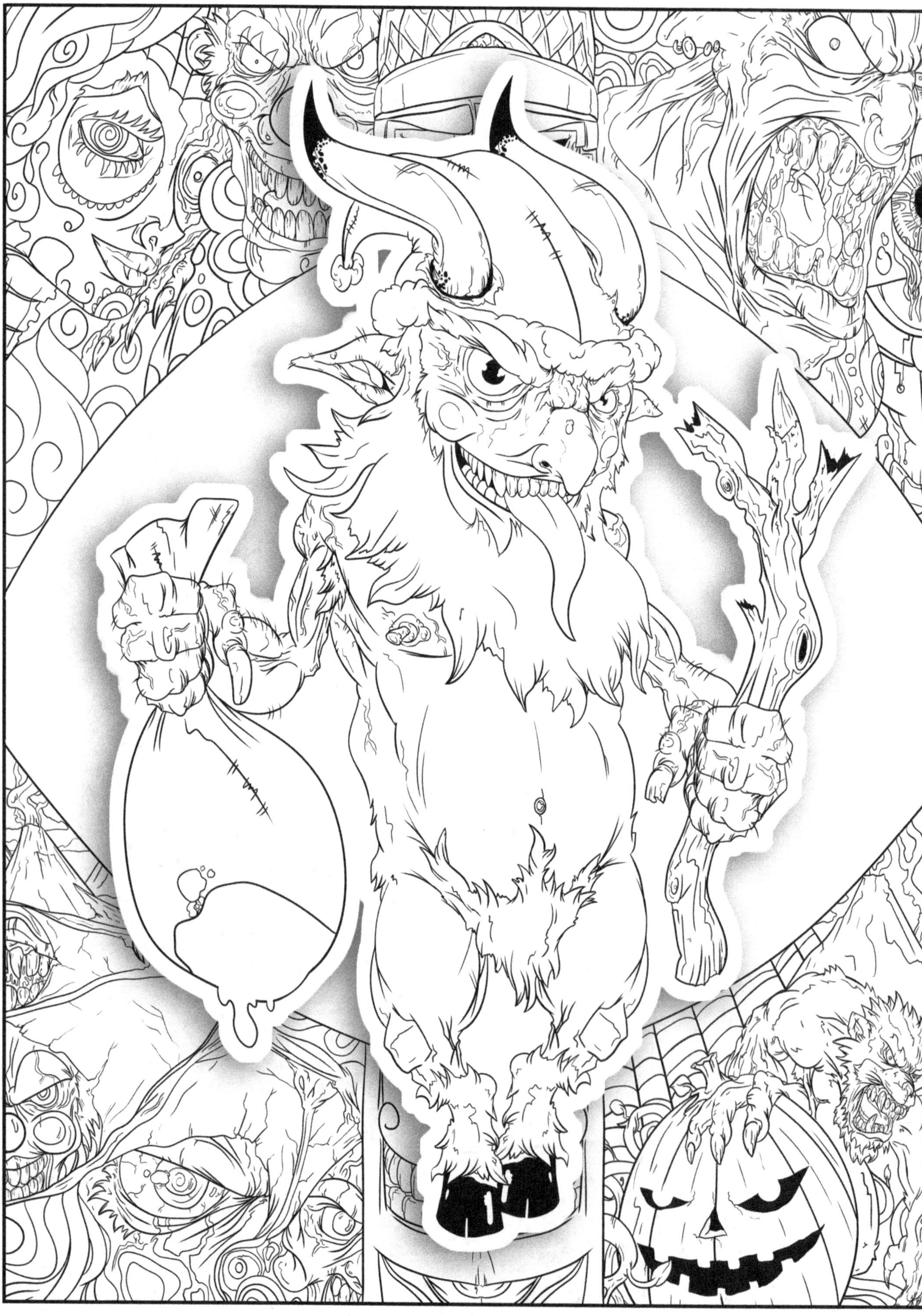

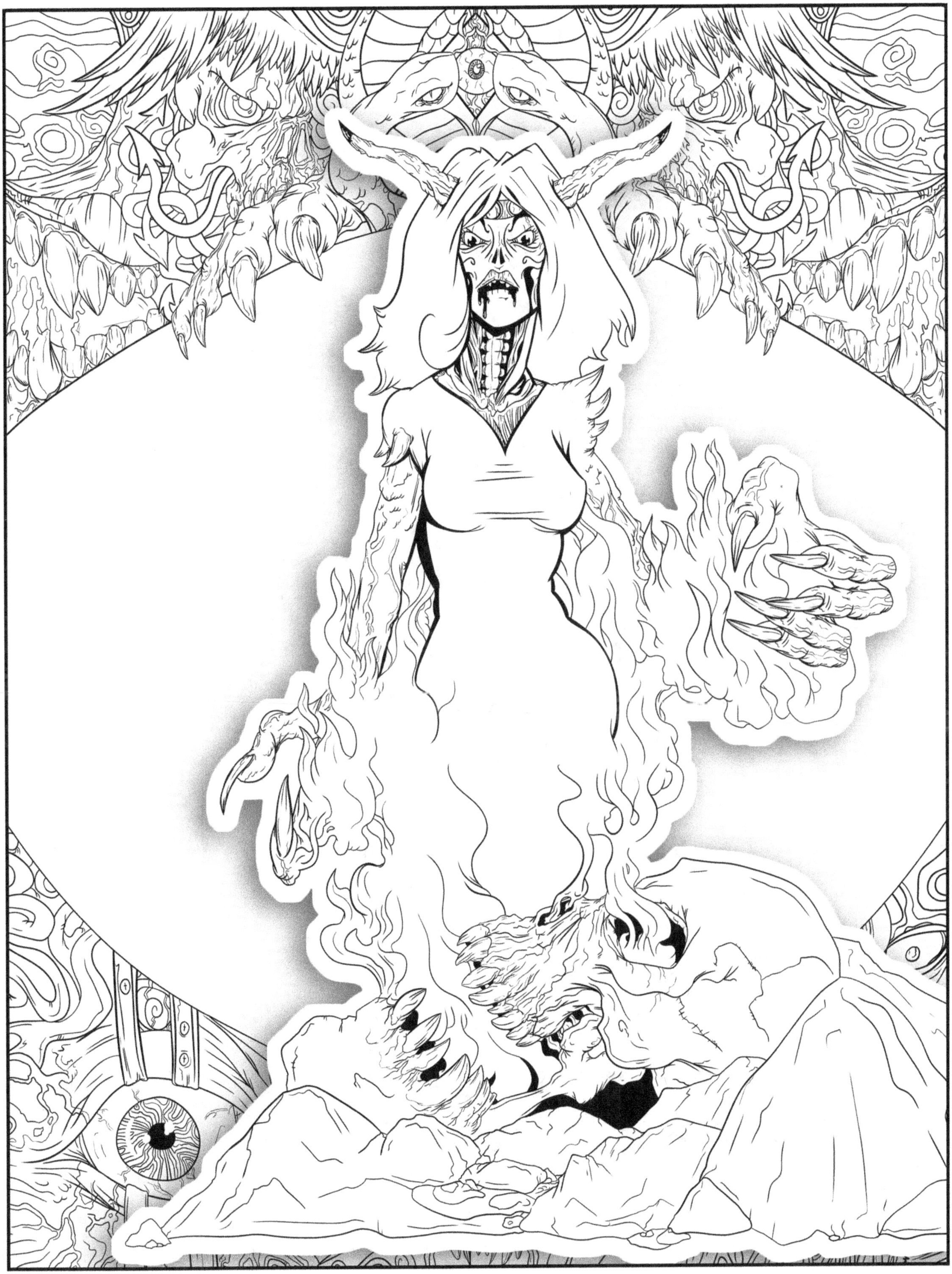

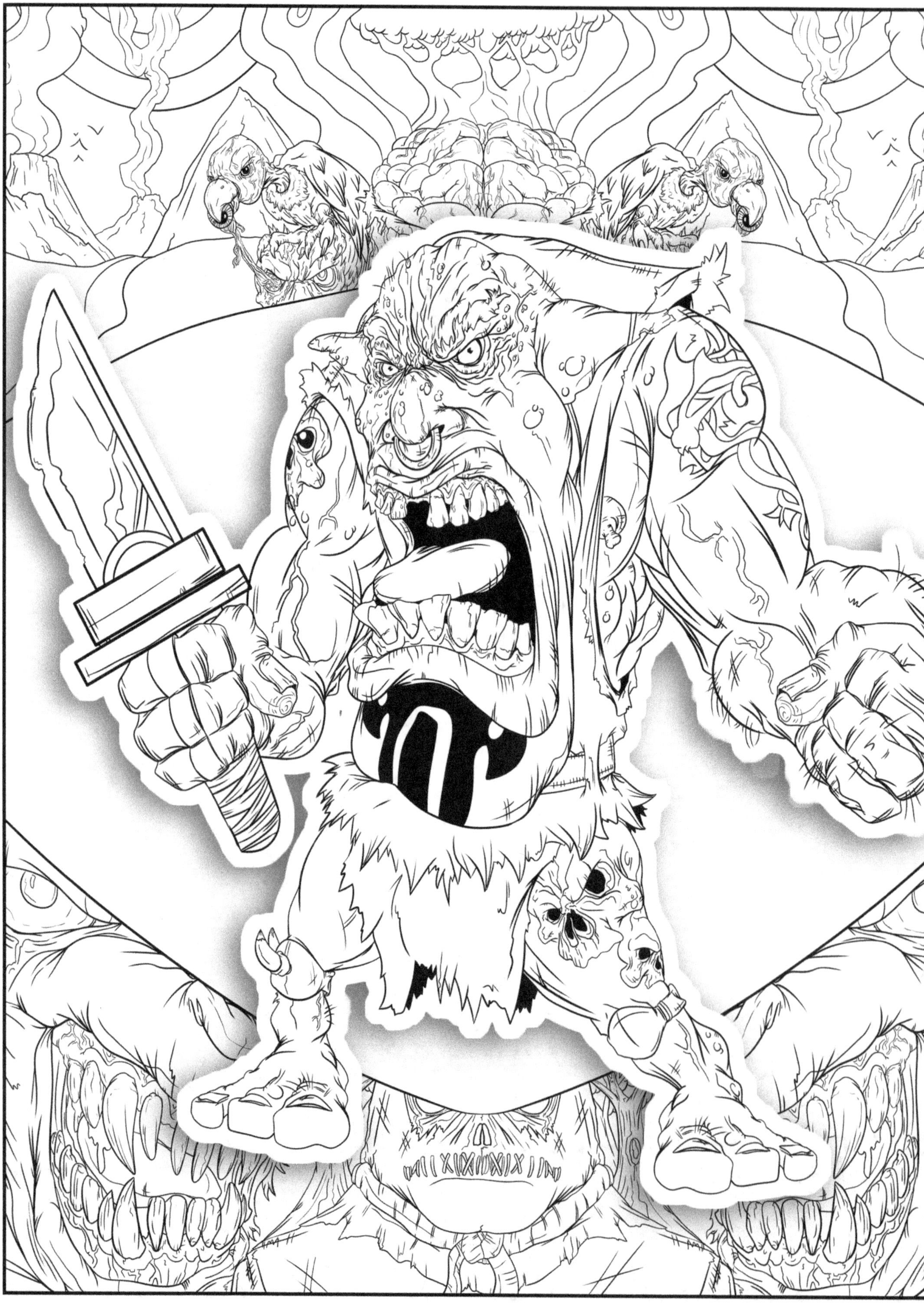

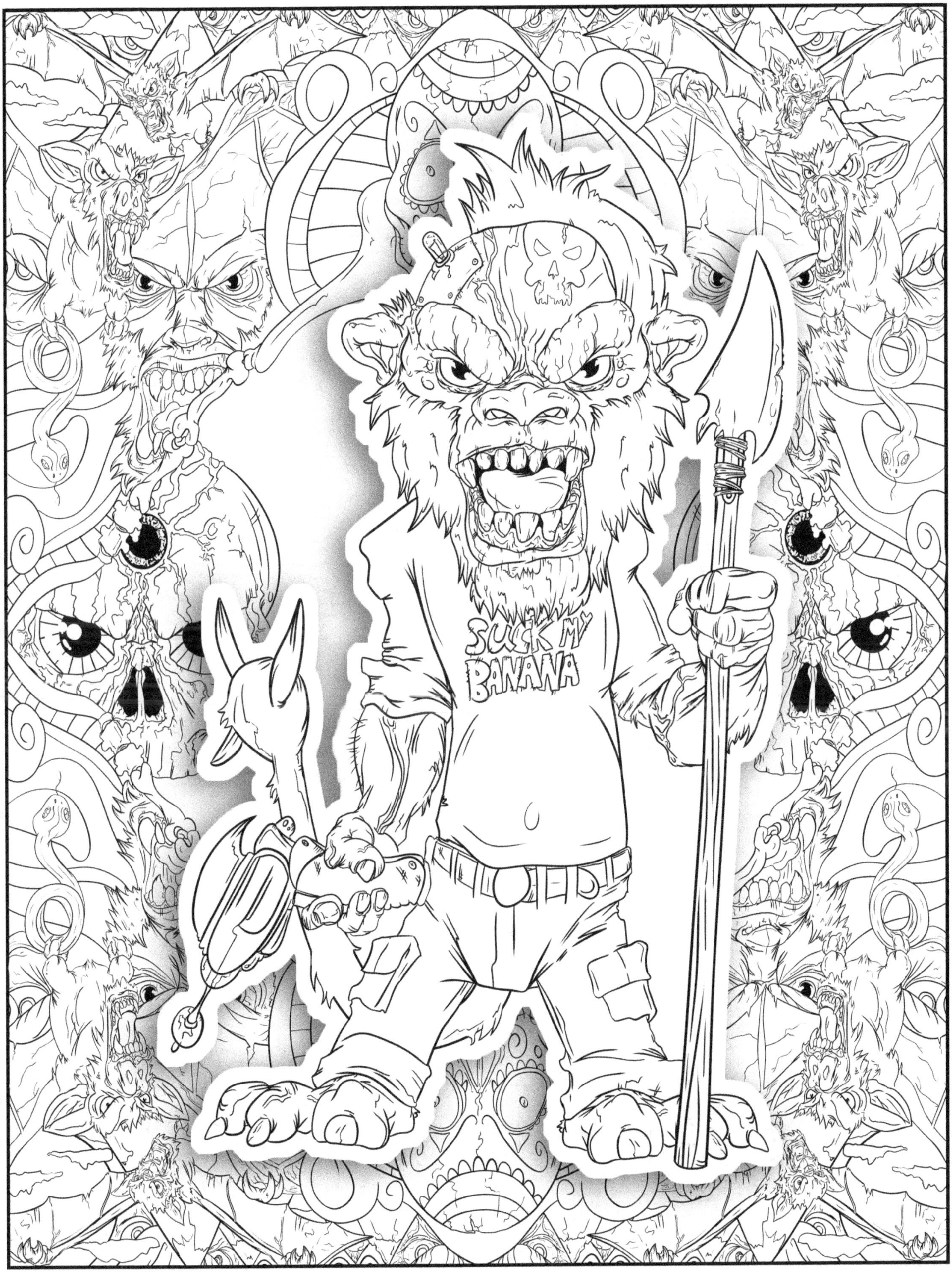
SUCK MY
BANANA

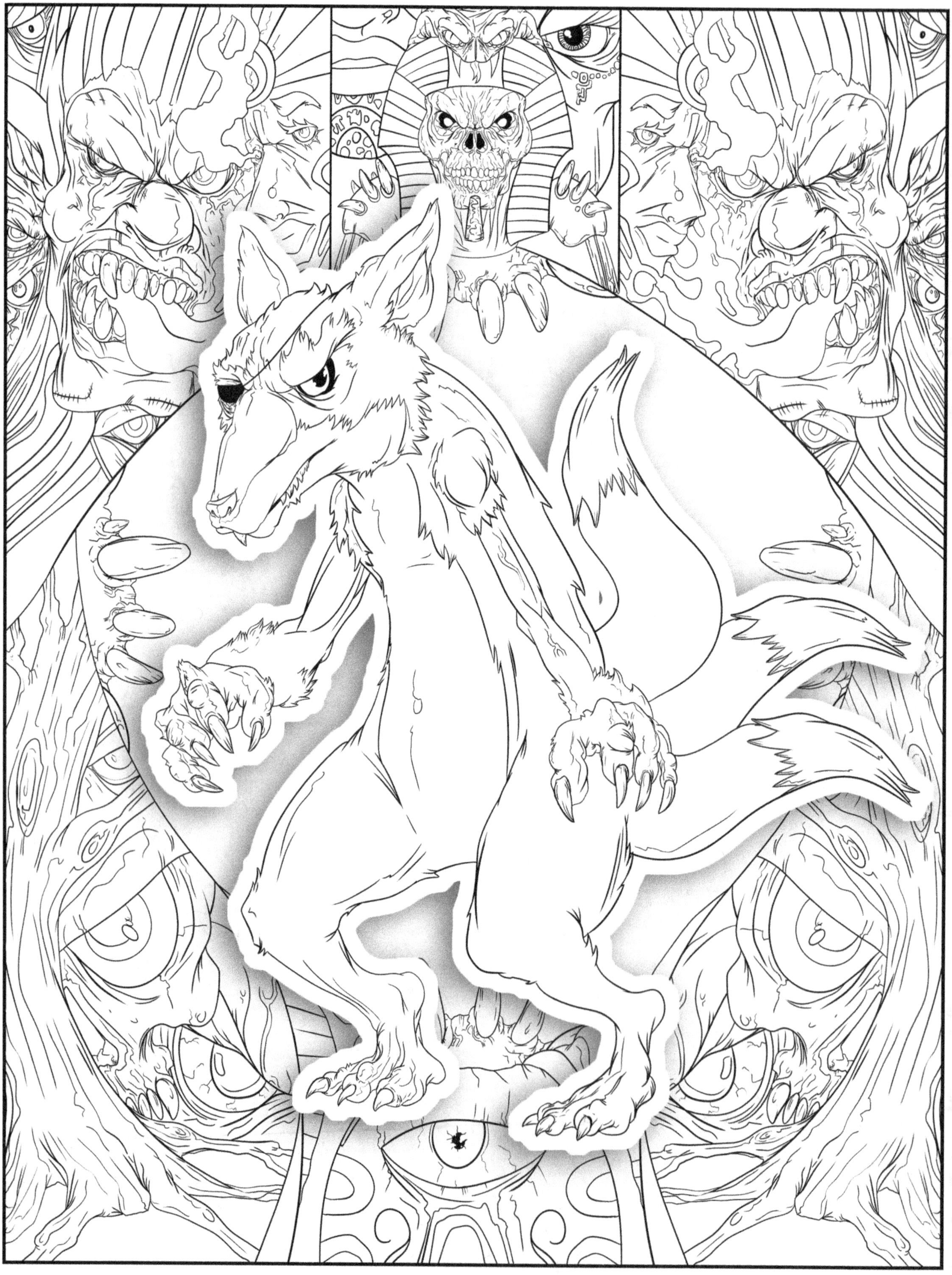

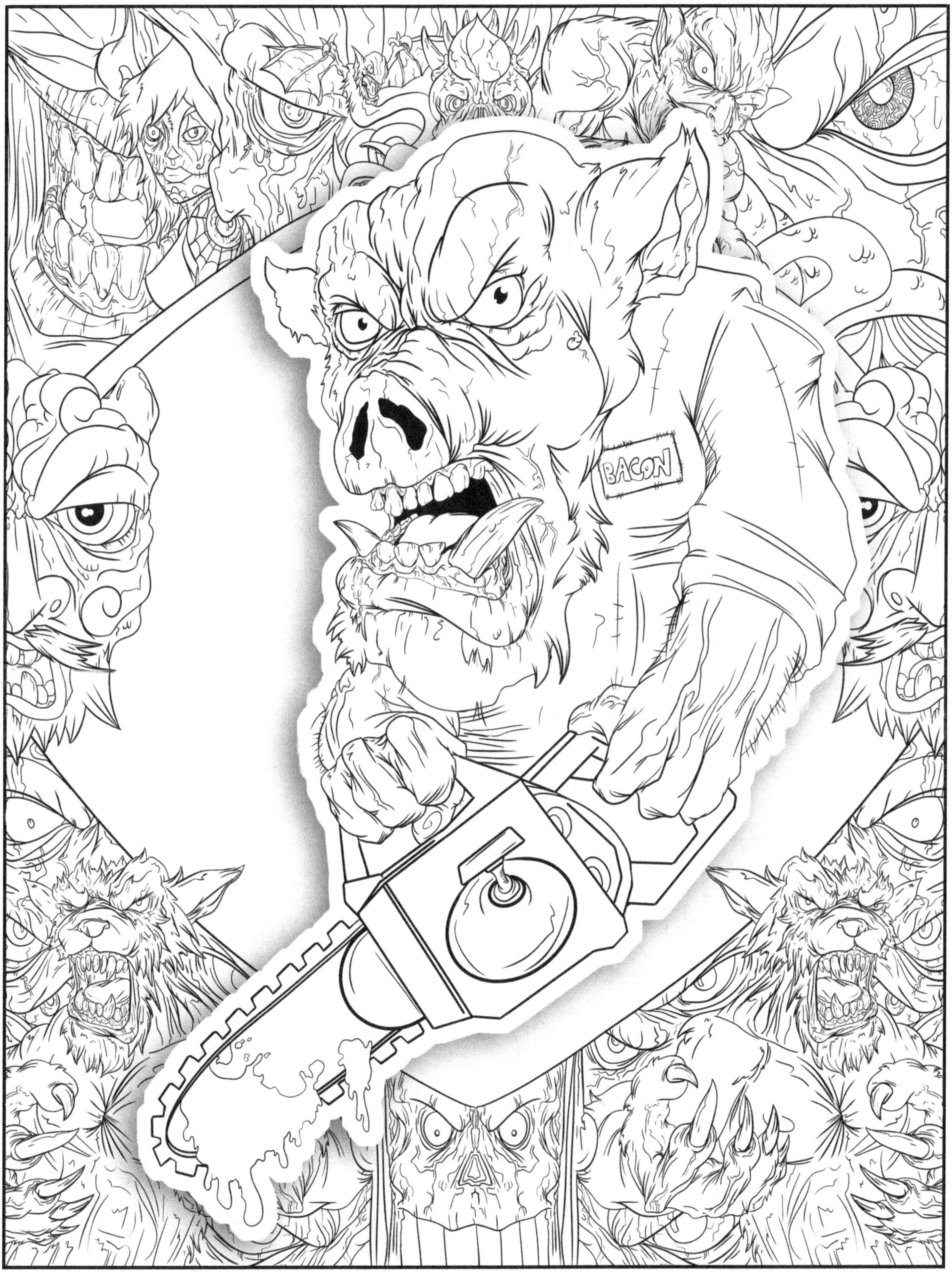
BACON

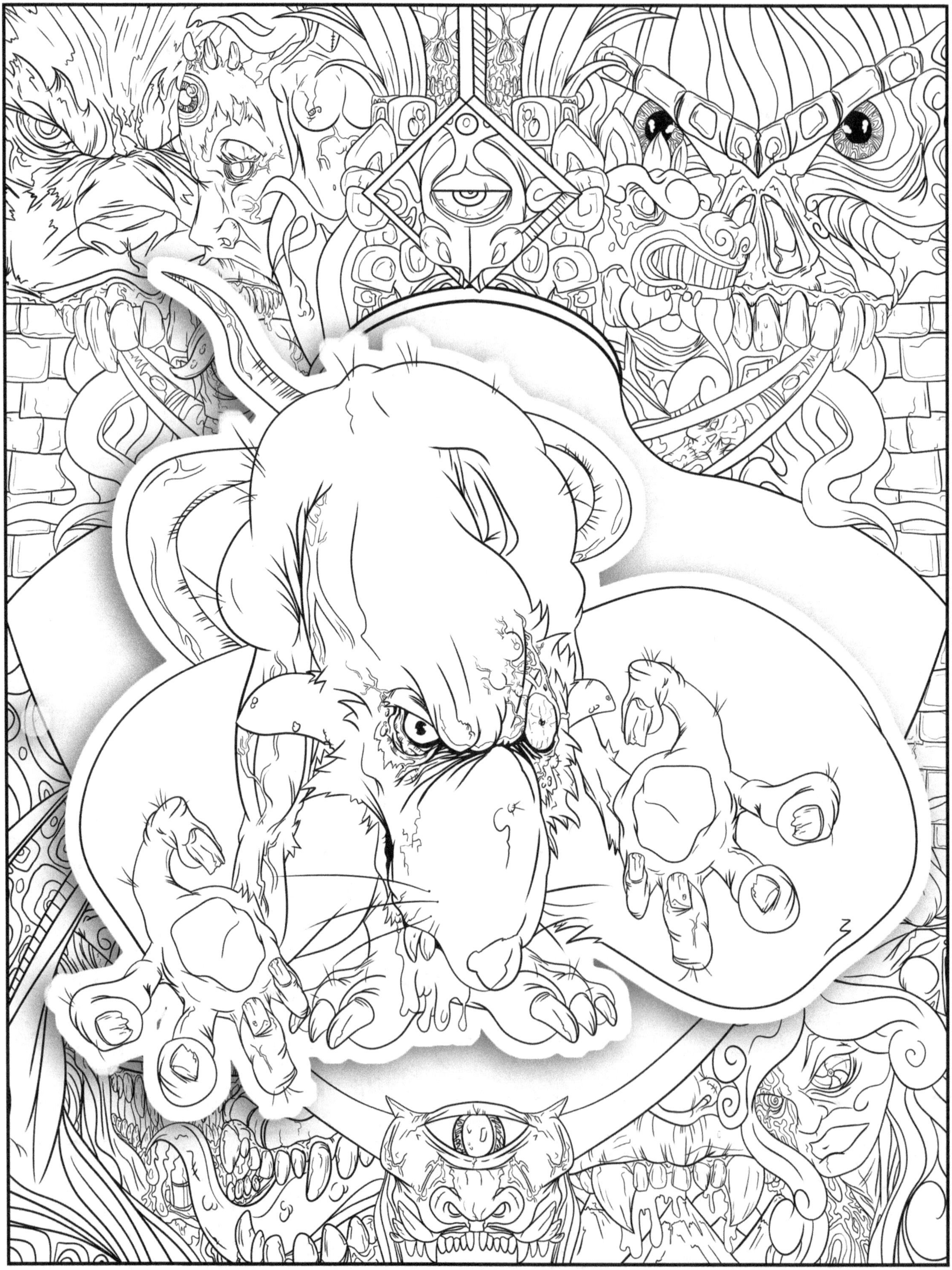

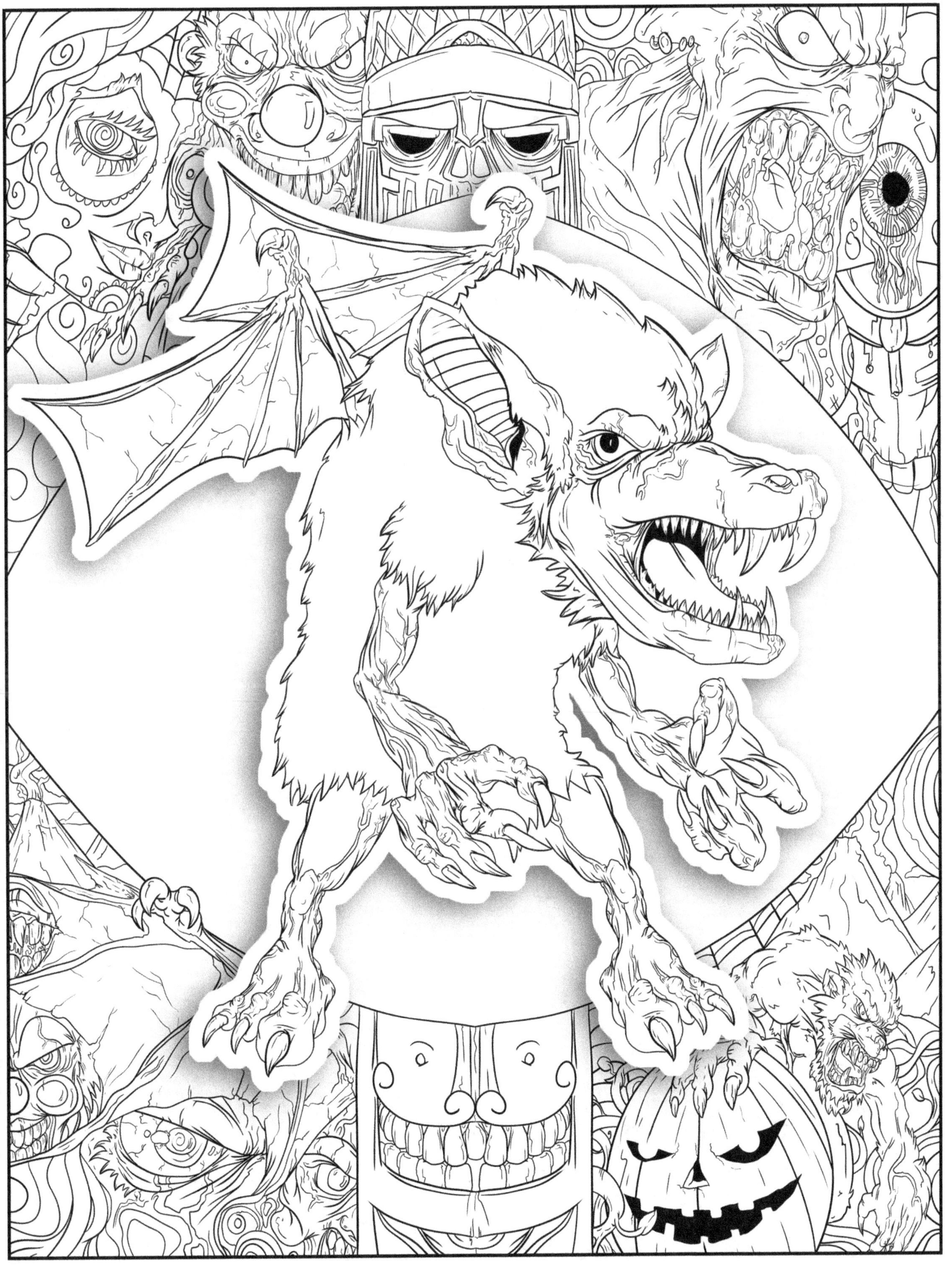

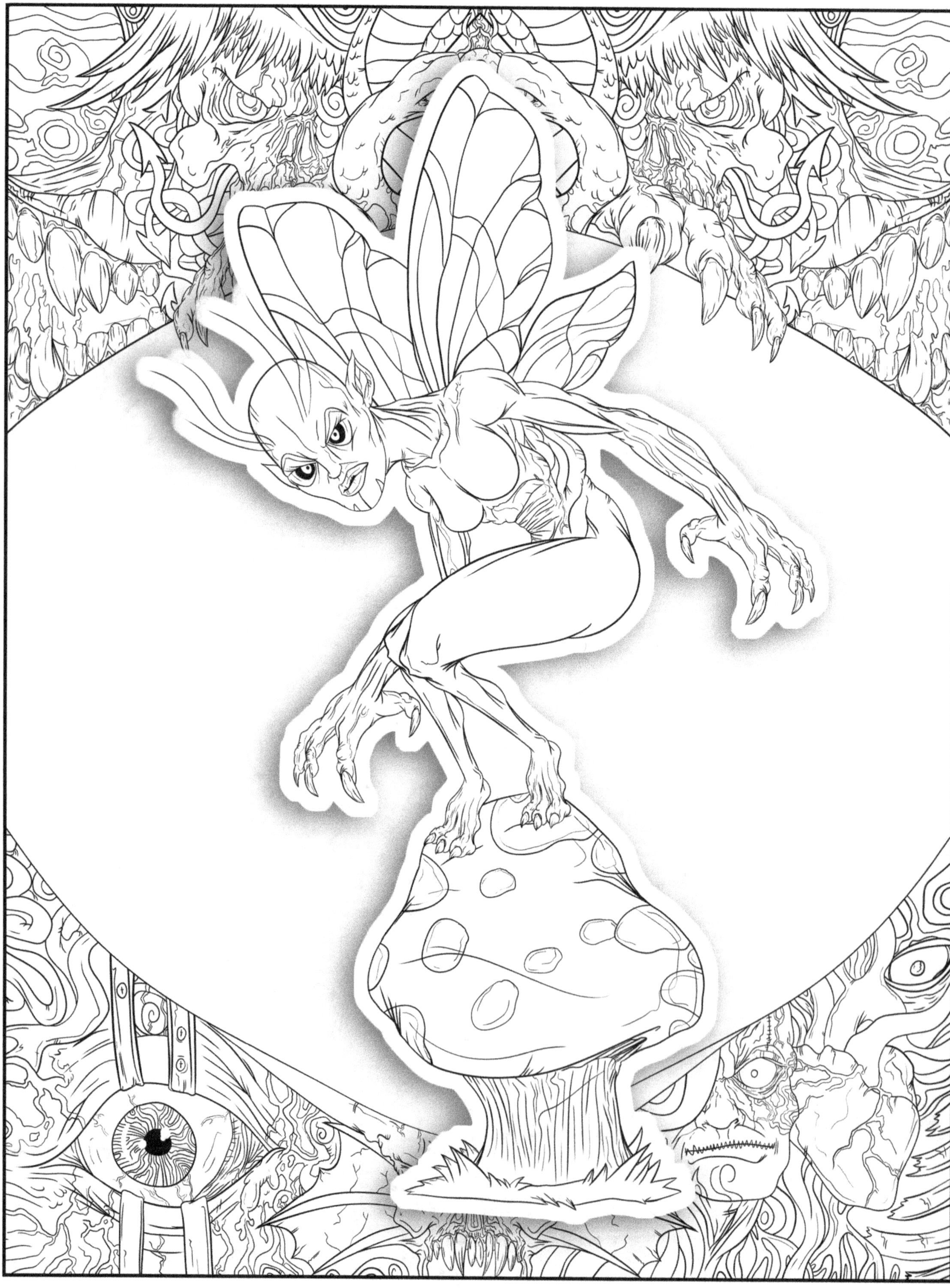

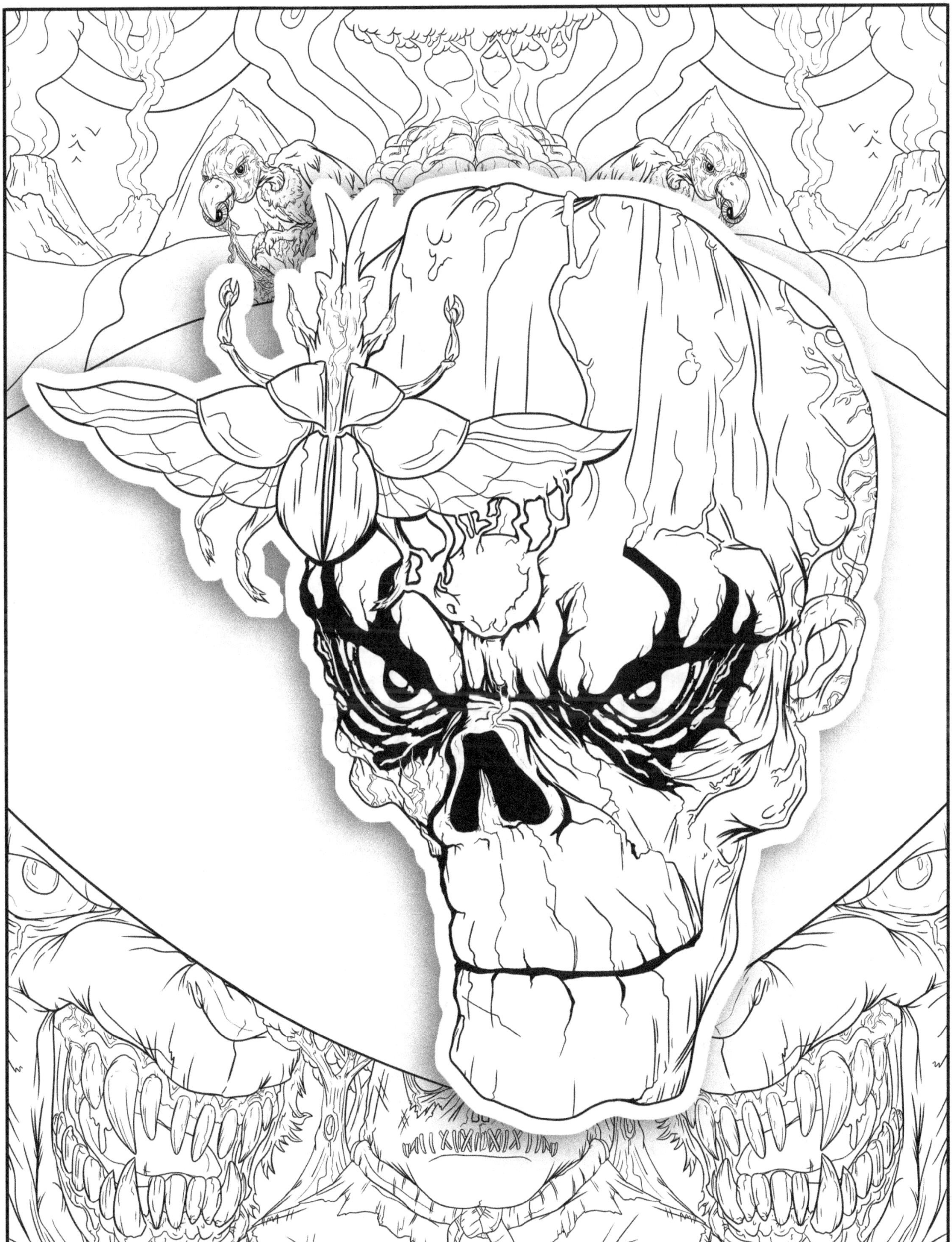

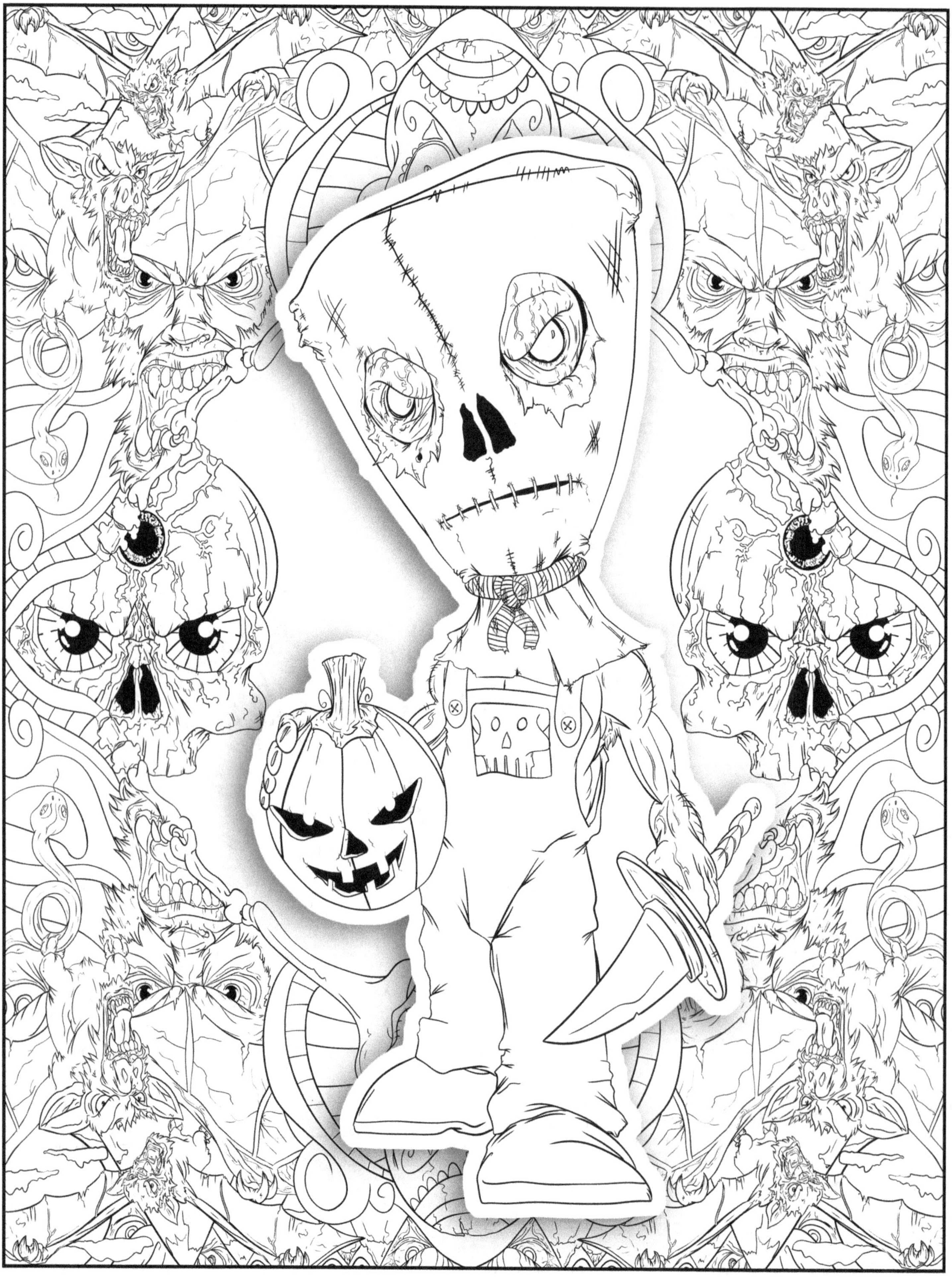

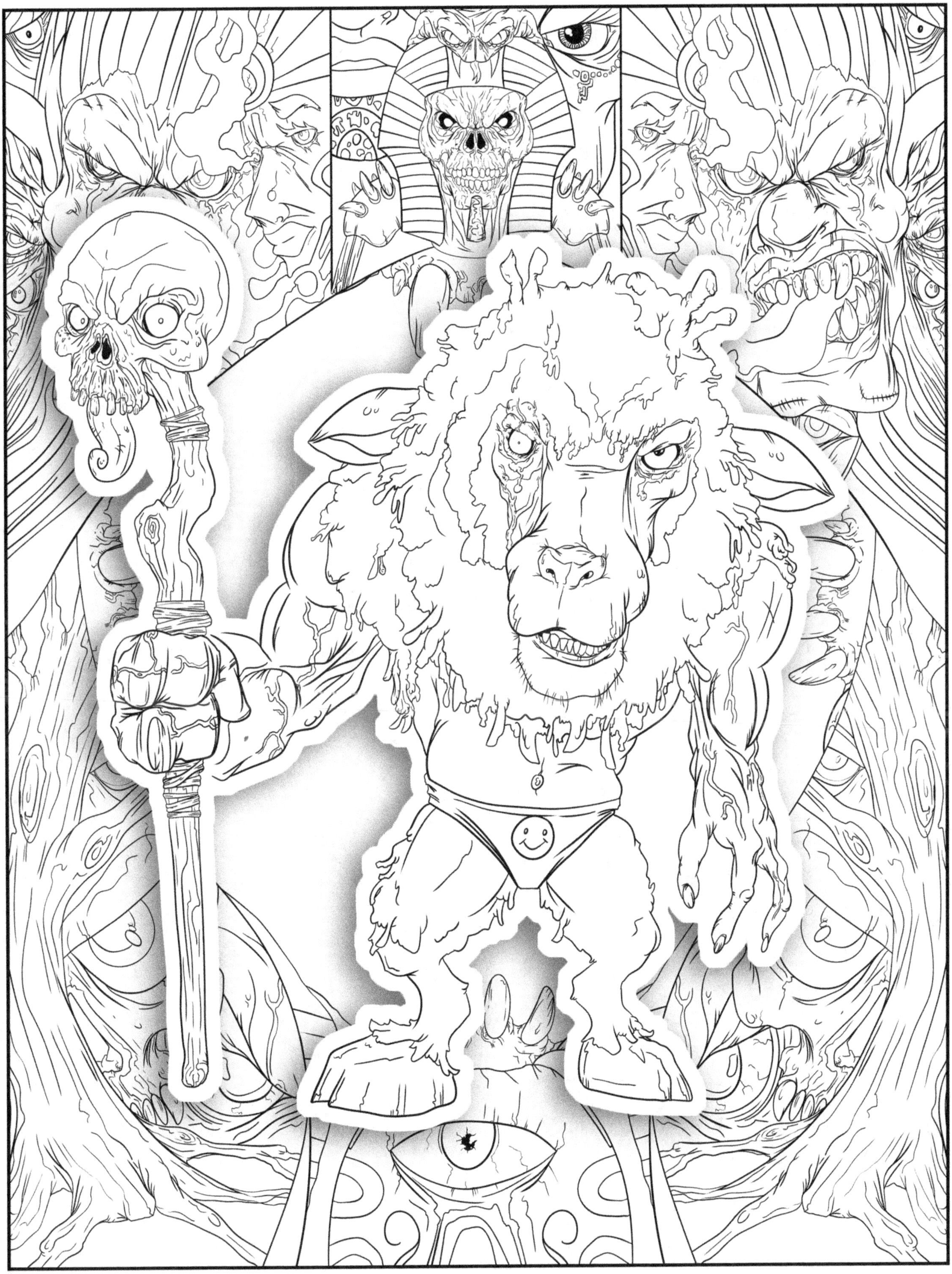

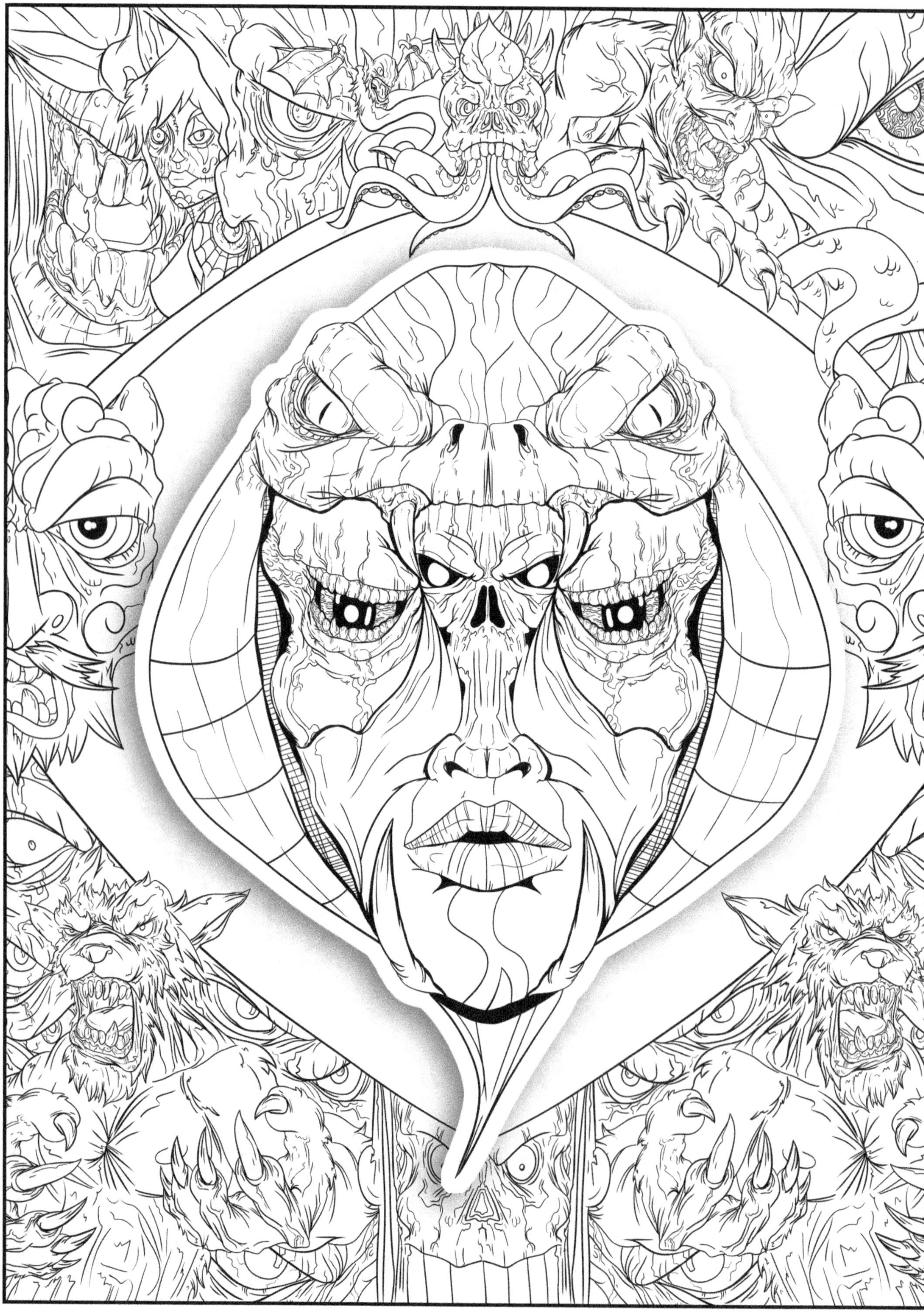

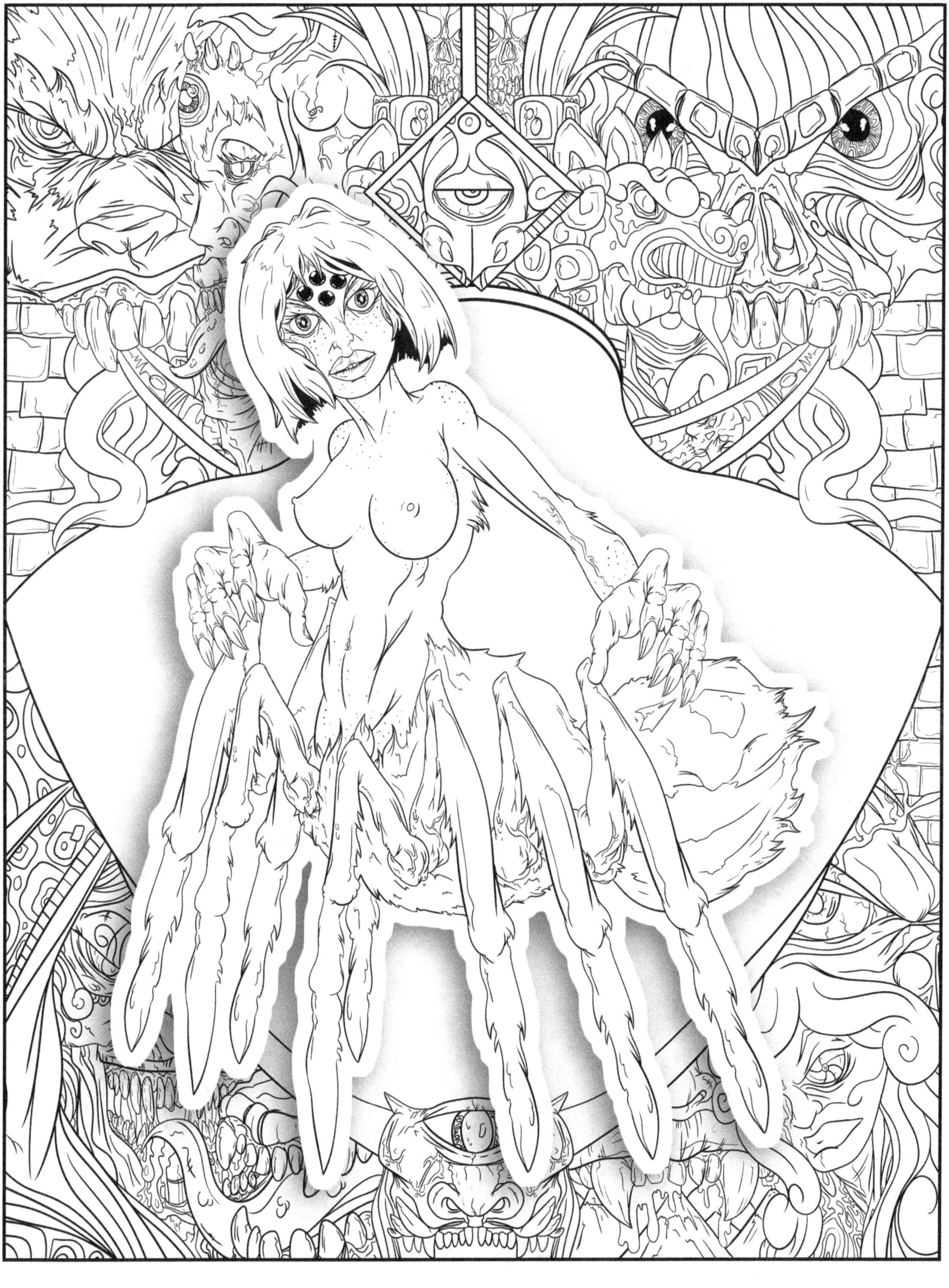

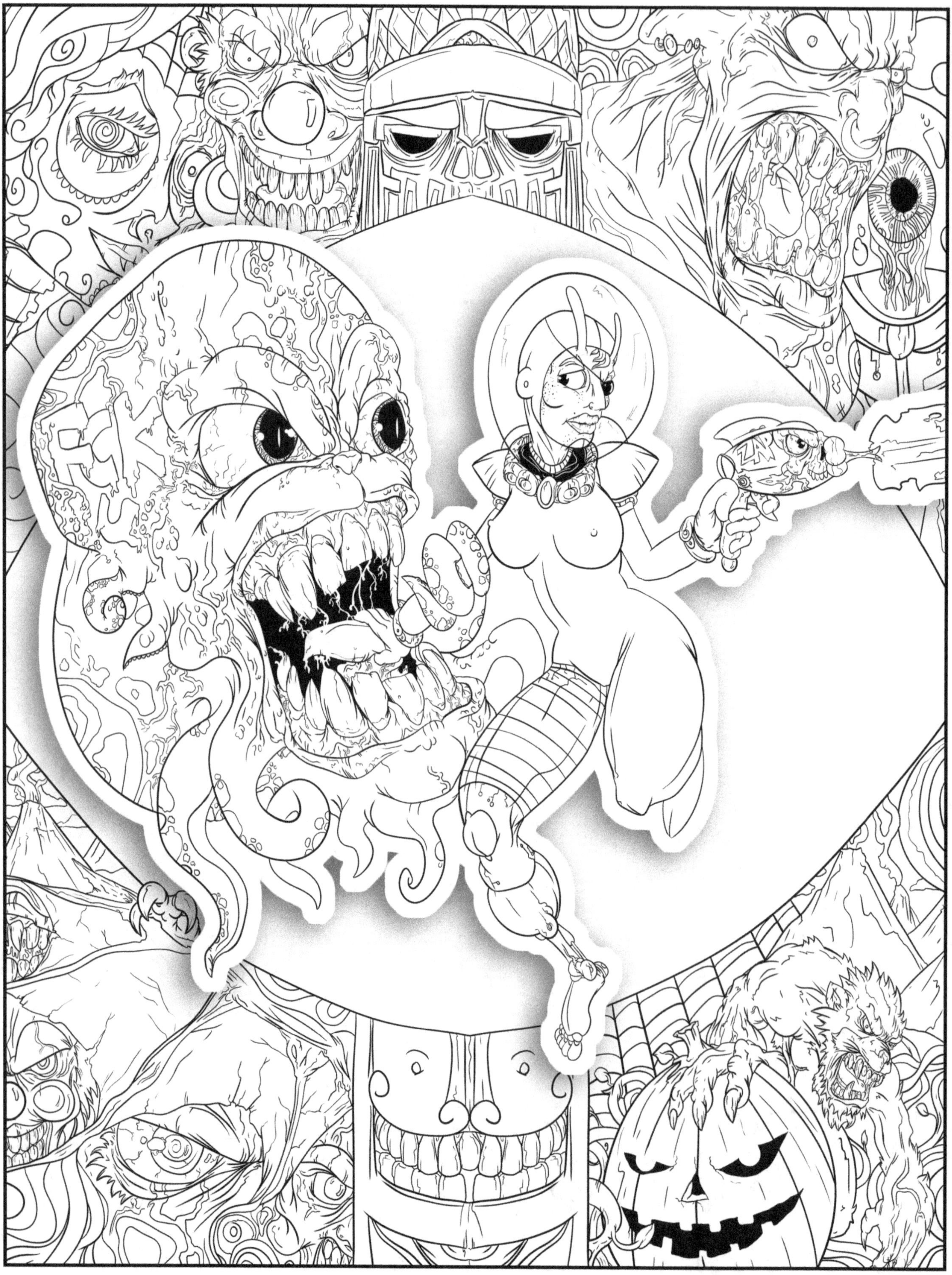

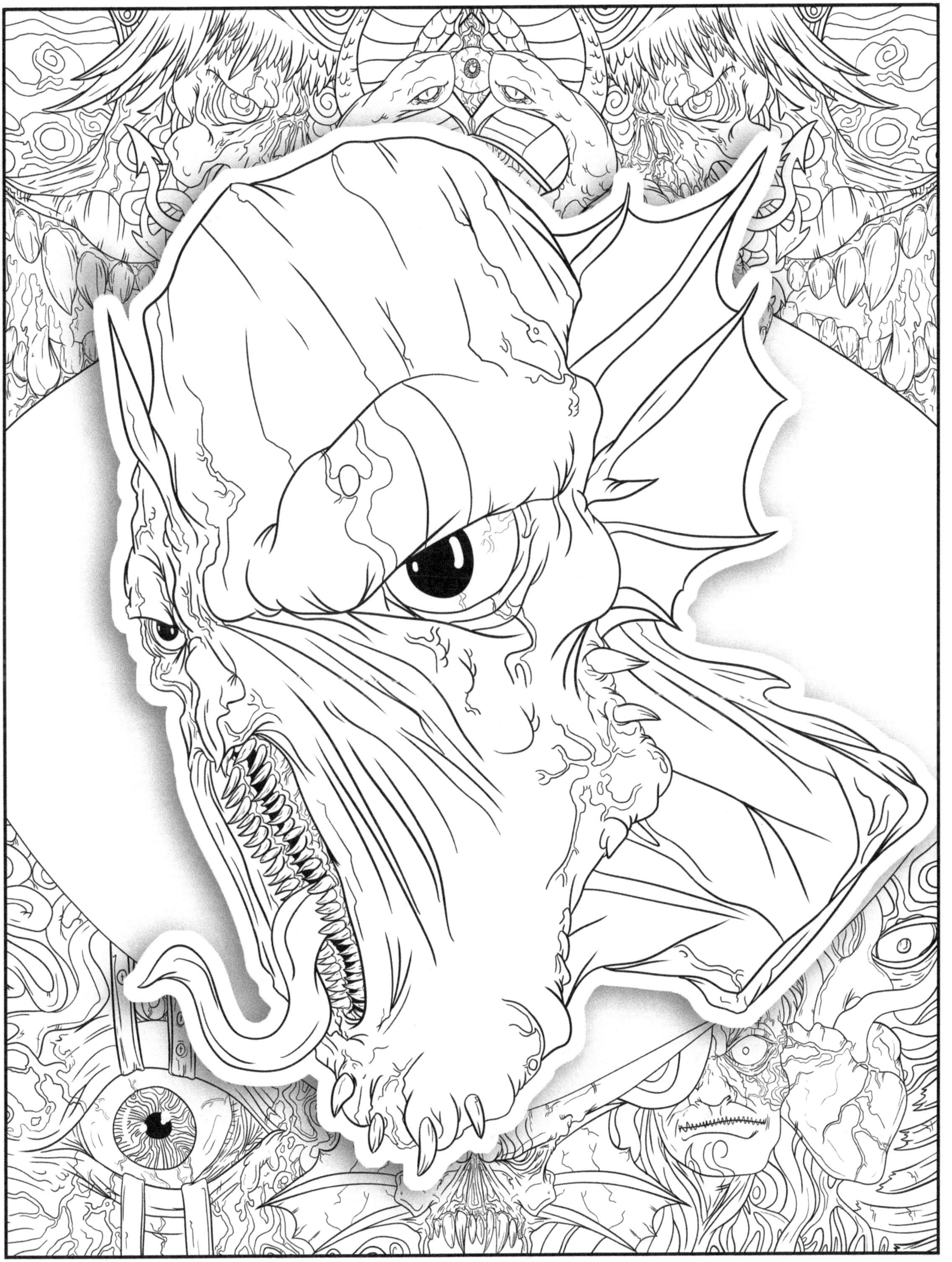

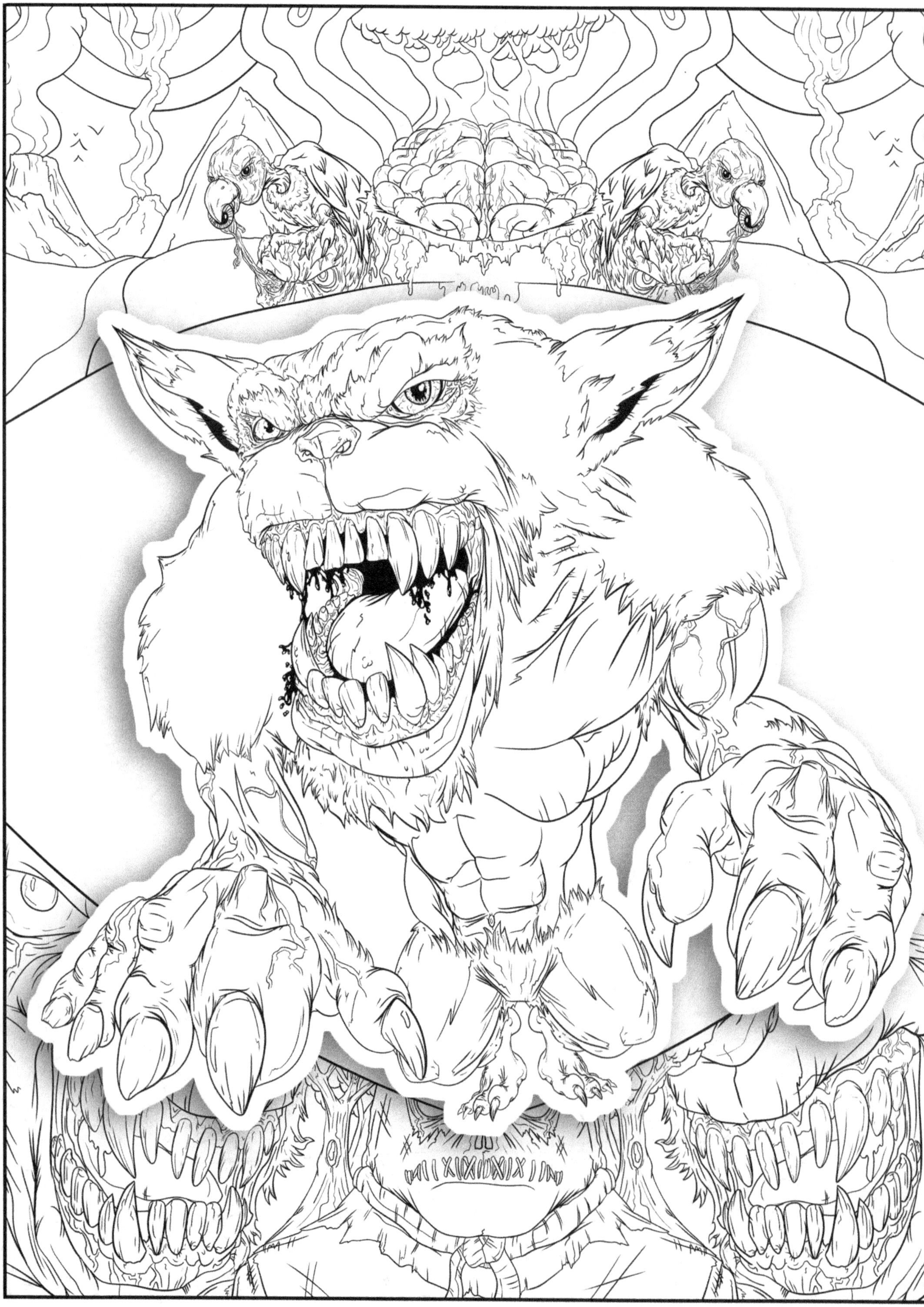

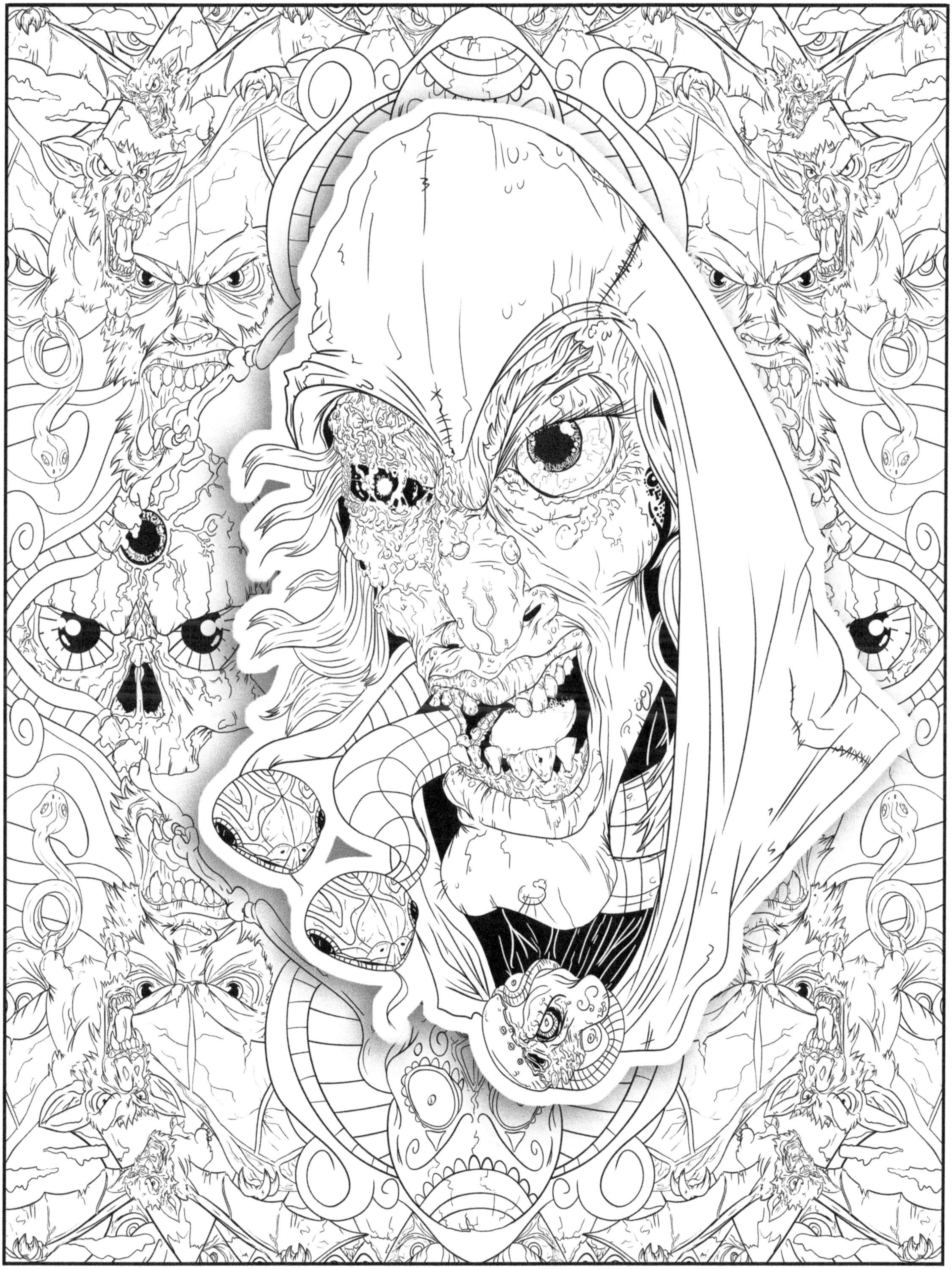

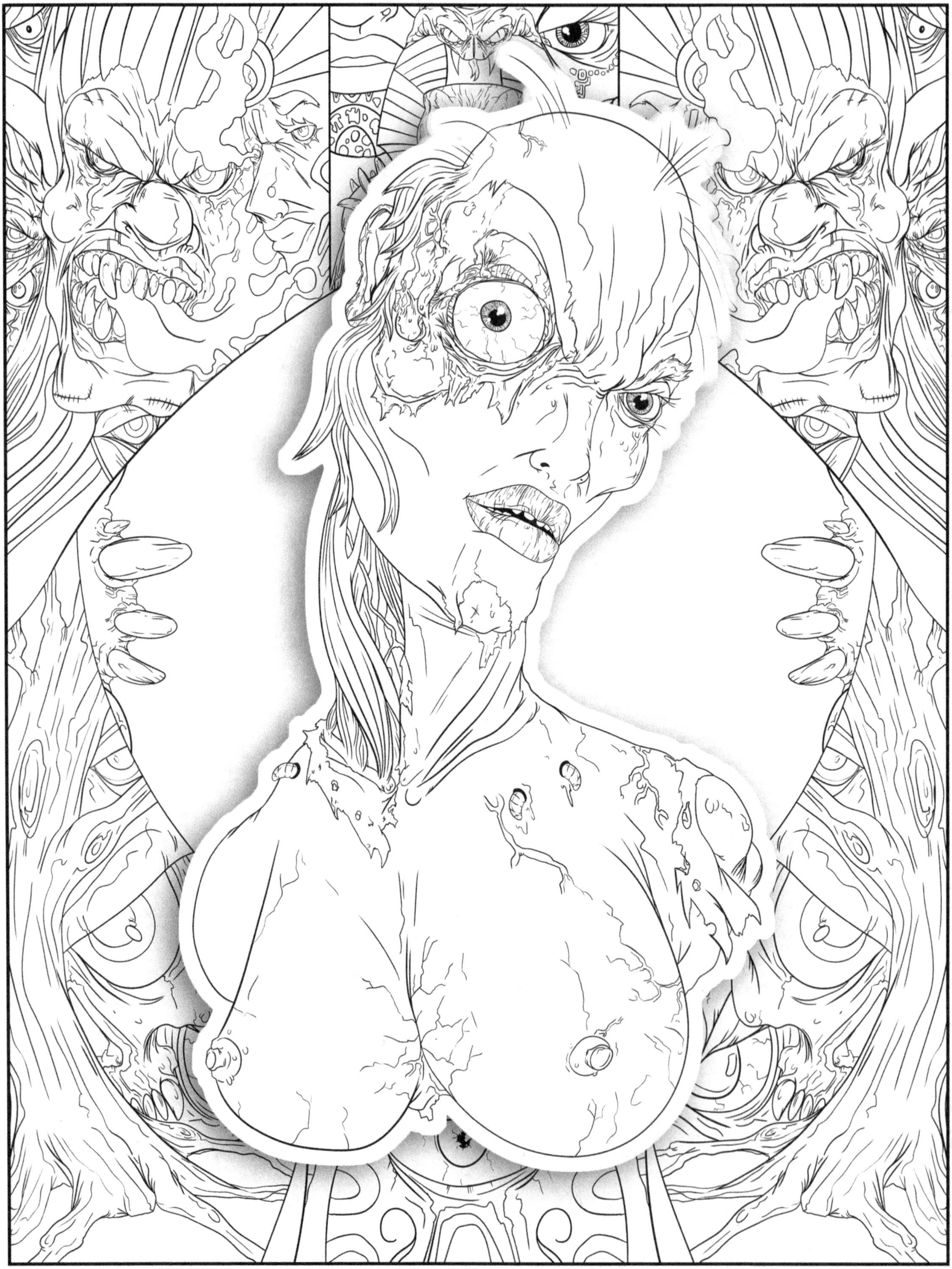

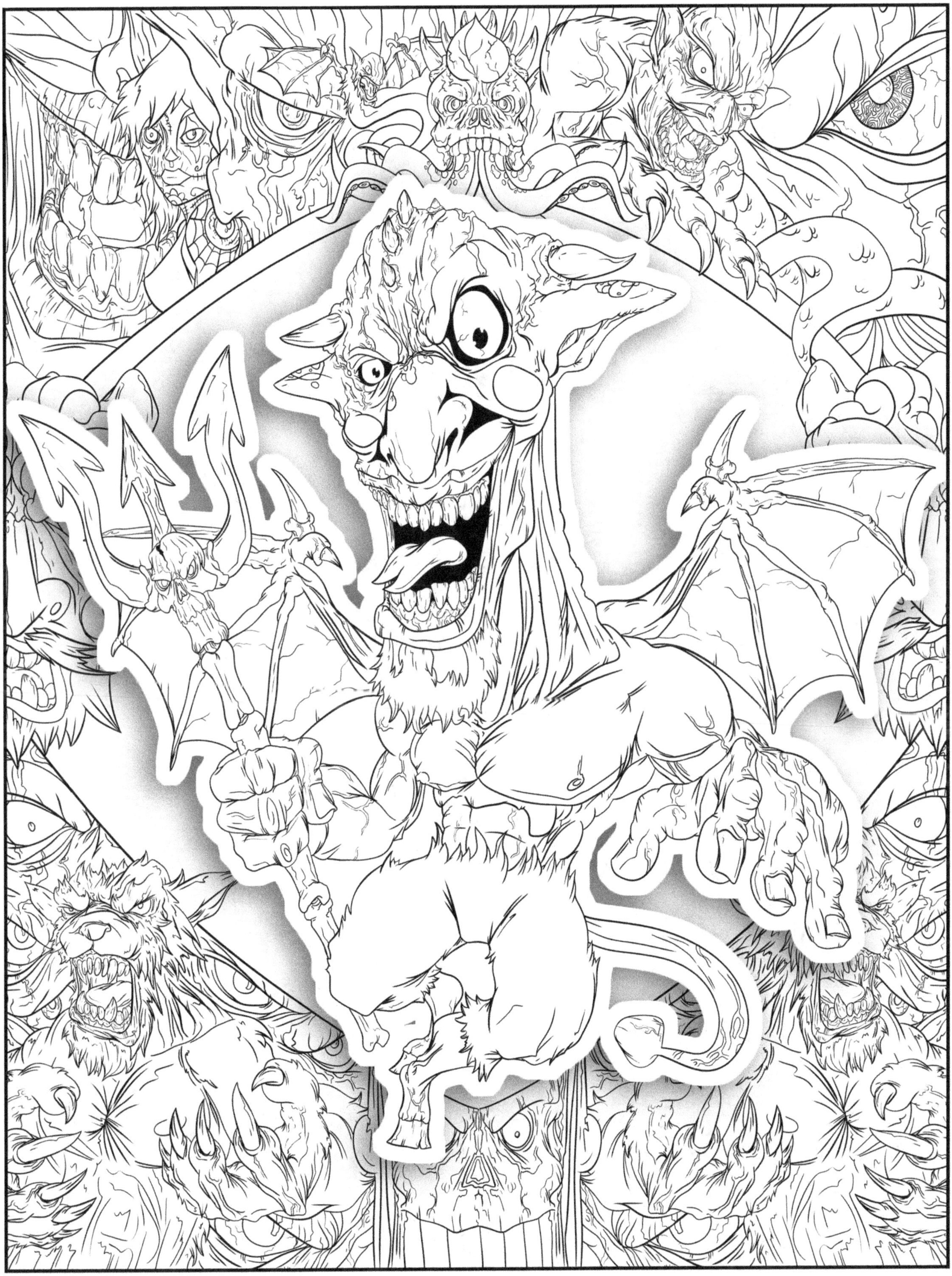

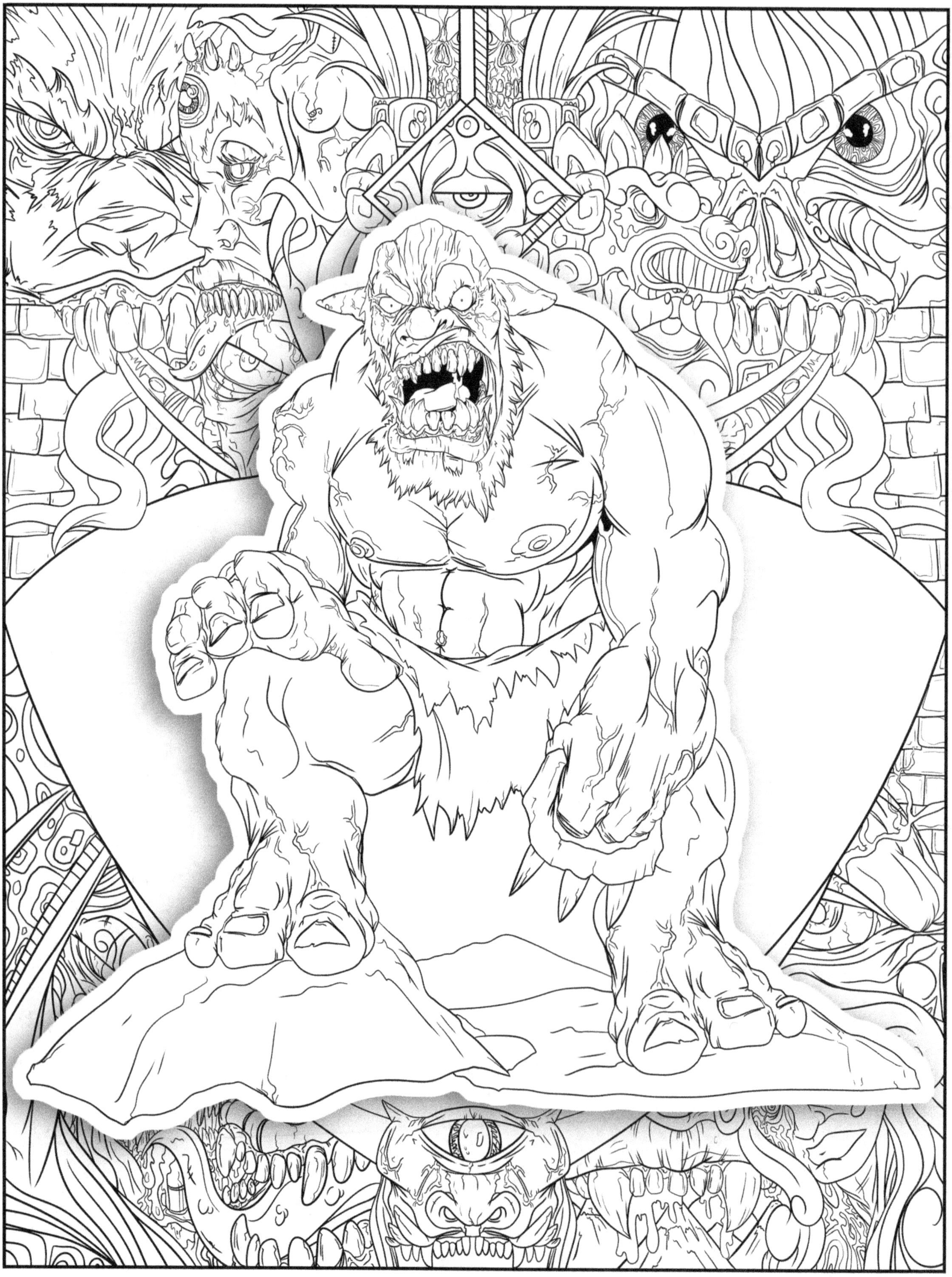

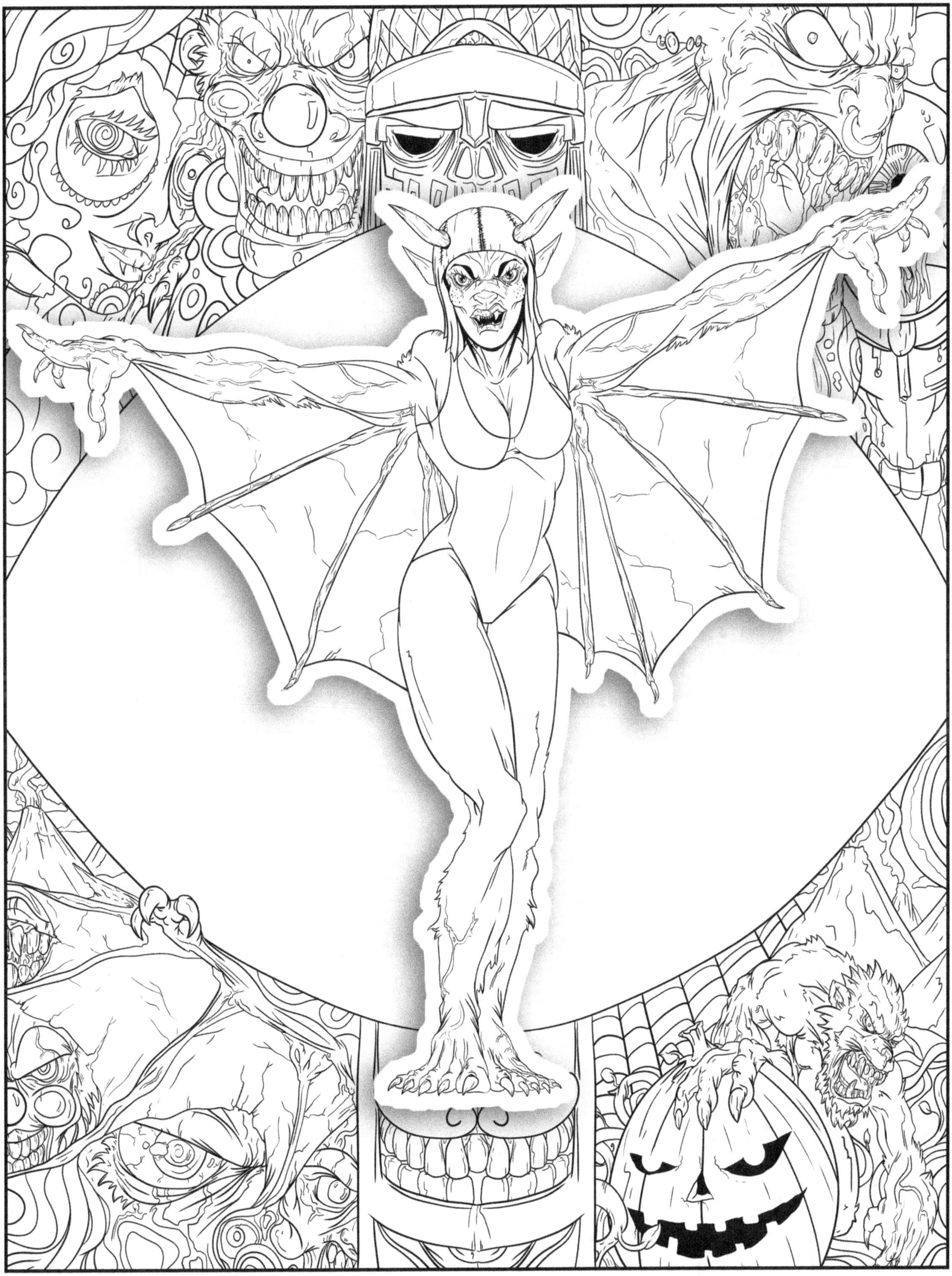

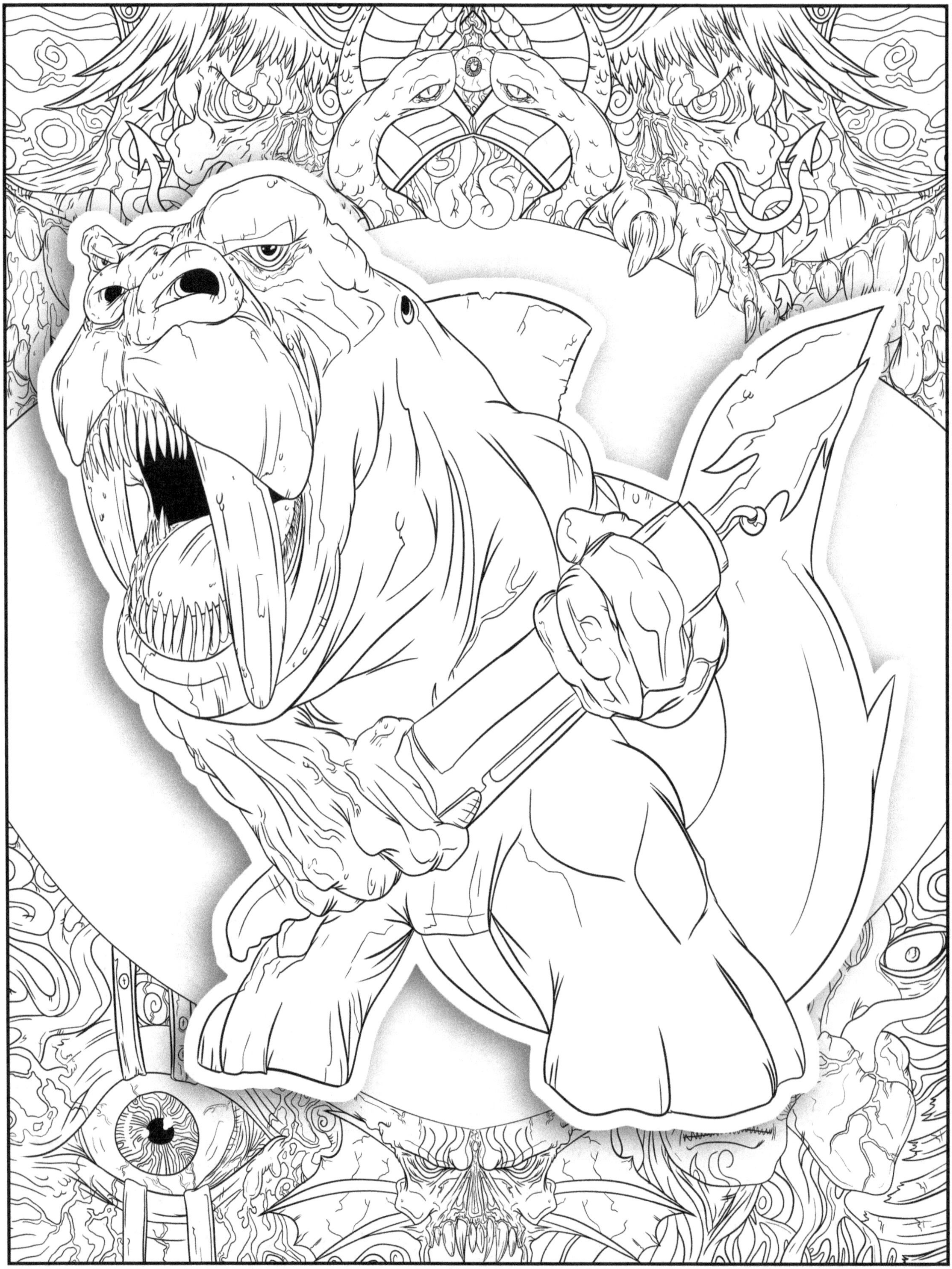

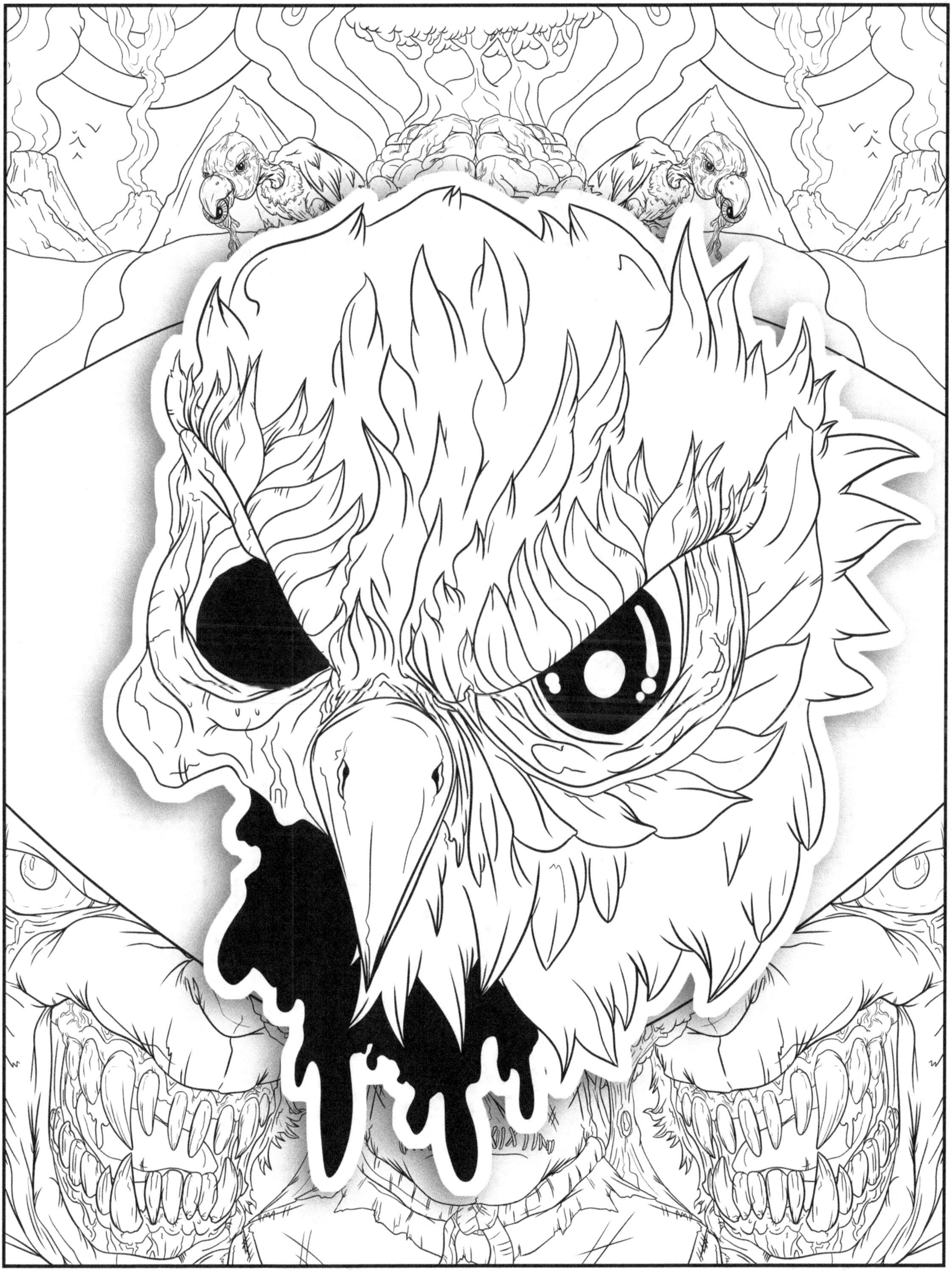

THANK YOU FOR COLORING

DARK LINES

BY: IAN MOSHER

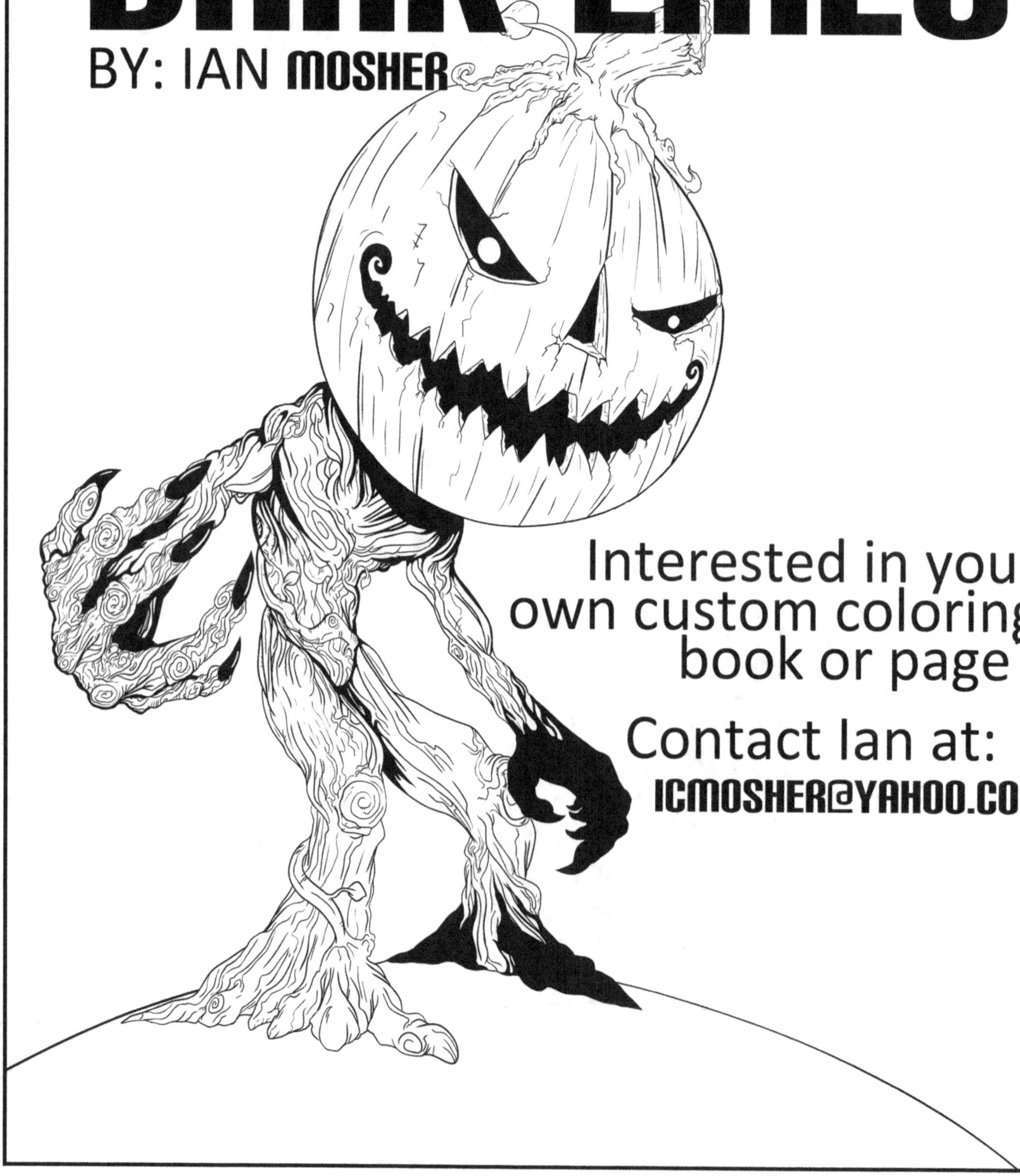

Interested in your own custom coloring book or page?

Contact Ian at:
ICMOSHER@YAHOO.COM

www.ingramcontent.com/pod-product-compliance
Lightning Source LLC
Chambersburg PA
CBHW081122240526
45470CB00019B/2921